About the Author

I was born in Newcastle in 1944, and as a child I caught Polio at 18 months old.

I became married in 1968 and divorced in 1990. I felt very fortunate to have had a daughter and two lovely grandchildren.

I still drive with disabled hand controls, visiting Southend, Epping Forest, The Old Mill and different parks, where I feel inspired to write, or also when I am listening to piano, violin or cello.

Many different spirits, guides or poets help with many of my writings. I have also been clairvoyant since 1979. Also, different artists have helped me with my paintings from a Chinese, Japanese, South or North American link, usually of an automatic nature.

I started to write after my friend Gwen passed to spirit, and after my spiritual experience with angels and healing. I know I experienced a miracle to help me within life and for others to benefit from it.

I have written this second book from my experiences within life.

Margie Anne

CHALLENGES WITHIN LIFE

AUSTIN MACAULEY
PUBLISHERS LTD.

A CIP catalogue record for this title is available from the British Library.

ISBN 978 1 78455 434 7 (Paperback)
ISBN 978 1 78455 436 1 (Hardback)

www.austinmacauley.com

First Published (2015)
Austin Macauley Publishers Ltd.
25 Canada Square
Canary Wharf
London
E14 5LB

Printed and bound in Great Britain

Contents

1
Will I Be Allowed...?

Will I be allowed to become born tomorrow?

This is what 'souls of spirit' are asking; for today and for future generations.

'Conception' will go through its natural course, if 'scientific ideas' are not put into peoples' minds to exterminate!

'Who are we to take away life
Before it has 'opportunity' to
Fulfil its growth or to
Know what colour eyes
'He' or 'she' is to have?

Just because 'some' do not
Wish to 'reap' what they sow
Only foolishness and heartache
Shall prevail...

Physical and mental disability is
Sometimes an embarrassment to
Others, who cannot always accept
Discomfort and ugliness.

So 'they' put in front of them: that
Easy way out.

'Abortion' is such a heavy mundane
Word, and should not be 'spoken'
Of lightly!

And only used in an 'emergency' or
If another 'life' has to become saved!
As a child would not be happy
Without its mother.

Babies and disabled people that
Fall into this category of
Being something different or
Something that has gone wrong
Within their make-up, surely
Should be allowed to breathe
Their own life! And for their
Own individuality to become 'acted' out!

To walk upon our own pathway…
We are tougher than you think!

Why should it be up to 'others' to
Have the last say?
For identity with purpose, we can achieve.

To 'use' our own 'initiative', then
'Compassion' on your part, to take
Over from pity…

A helping hand is sometimes all that
Is needed to get us from A-B
And not to 'conform' to
Your way of thinking!

The opposite is usually true,
We might 'appear' stubborn to
Some people's eyes! Because
'We' are not losers, 'we' need to
Stay winners!

The 'weaker part of our shell' may
Need 'aids' to strengthen or
To hold us upright! For 'us' to walk!

And for brushes to be 'placed' within
Our mouths; so some of 'us' are
'Able' to paint
'Pens' to become 'placed' within our
Toes... 'Guide Dogs' to become that
'Light' for the blind!

So our courage has to stay strong!
Some of 'us' hold that inner
Knowledge for creativity, art, music
And poetry...

And an appreciation for many
'Blessings' that we have!

For what we lack, we try to 'use'
To the best of our ability, so
Should not become hidden
Behind tears and self-pity.

For you find the more disabled
A Person is... the 'happier' their spirit!

As 'healing' for our mental and
Physical state, can become found.
If we have 'faith' and to
Know that 'God' would not ask
Too much of us?
For our lives would become
'Shortened' if the 'need' arose.

So 'allow' God to have the last
Word, for 'He' is the creator
Of all life and we're sure that
'Abortion' is not within 'His'
Vocabulary.

We may not 'appear' pretty to some
Sometimes we must be a bind!
Usually we are more sensitive than
Others, so we 'learn' to use our
'Personality' within our own 'misfortunes'.

With the 'opportunity' to 'use' it wisely
And with confidence.

For within 'God's' eyes He will give
'Us' that 'inner strength' with
An 'olive branch' to lift 'our
Spirit' when needed.

Then!
To help 'us' along the way.

***

From 'my own experience' as a child Polio victim

2
One Lonely Indian

One lonely native Indian
Sitting upon a mountain plain;
So high – so magically near to
The sky!

Thinking very deep – sitting 'upon'
His bare back horse
And with huge birds of those
Clouds looking down upon those
Distant valleys… at 'white
Man' and to what they might
Bring…?

As 'contempt' hurts their grieving eye
For 'willing damage' is 'all'
What 'they' bring.

For 'they' do not hear 'God' sing
Amongst mountain country; or
To hear echo cries… amongst
Our lands of peace.

Some only wish to destroy!
And for 'our people' to
Turn into ash
And for 'our bison' to become
Extinct.

***

Native American Indians are very close to me due to
influences from 1800's communication.

3
We Are Capable of Love?

Are we still waiting for that love to
Reach out towards us…
To confirm that we are capable of
Being loved, within life's journey?

Maybe we have just 'accepted' those
Little things of life. Felt content, until
A loneliness chased us.

For if we like to sing with bird echoes
As well as the treasure of flower perfume,
We know nature has been on our side.

Courage we can receive from that humble!
Tree; for our faith might hold strong,
But we still need that soul friend,
At the end of a day – to colour; to
Give that second opinion.

For our pathway can seem bumpy,
Maybe the odd pebble or two
So finding someone with a similar smile
To go that extra mile…
Sharing two heartbeats within this
Mighty world
Is much better than staying alone.

4
Breaking Away From Chains

We often wonder when real happiness will
Redeem itself
For we know we can survive when
Creation, growth with nature is there
In front of our eyes! For us to
Sense its perfume everywhere.

For then, our own emotions 'dance'
With bird, butterfly and moving tree,
Their leaves singing a song!
For with passing clouds, darker skies
Can make our heart feel heavy
And sullen.

We might give a sigh, then say "Oh
Well, life's not that bad really?"
For if 'faith' can move mountains
Then we can hold on until new
Sunrise echoes its glory!

Breaking away from binding chains
That became so tight around our
Ankles, our wrists
For with patience
We shall have discovered
Our freedom, upon…

Our new pathway that is yet to become
Finally shown.

***

From my own experience with life

5
God's Little Flowers

Long stemmed flowers
Happy within a vase
Appear so radiant, so extra, so colourful!
For they reflect light, that has
Become 'dormant' within each soul.

For if we were to 'hold' just one strong
Bloom closer towards our heart
Lonely forgotten tears would be able
To flow freely.
Allowing their own perfume to kiss
You.

With a reminder that we are 'one'
Of the creator's precious smaller flowers
Needing to become nurtured
And adored.

For sometimes this world seems
So empty…

Until our own growth 'blossoms' or
Within God's earthly garden.

6
Take a Broad Look

Take a broad look into your life
That has been 'giving' to you
Always look at your sad times
Not with tears…
But to find a way to 'new awakenings'
That have been 'hidden' from view.

For your downfalls might seem
Your weaker side, but we can
Come up fighting at the end
Of your day.

So allow courage to become your
Master, pushing 'unwanted' thoughts away…
Then, become ever grateful
That you can 'speak' within a
Peaceful prayer.

And that all the days of pain; were
Learning days
Encouraging another page of your
Spiritual book to become written…
And had finally become
Your gain!!

7
Life is Like a Tapestry

Our life is like a tapestry blended
With colour and shape
That can 'appear' bright and
Loving, or sometimes sullen
With 'mistakes' that we make.

Some days we might appear 'open'
To the blueness of blue sky
Then we walk away from
Helping hands – yet cannot
Give a reason why?

For pity can lead to 'self-destruction'
Then stitches within life, can
Drop one-by-one
It's only when we decide to pick
Them up... do we realise that
A learning stage has just begun.

For new cottons can become 'woven',
Making a new tapestry
Needing our lives to come alive
So others might notice hidden
Talents, expressed in what they see.

Then we can say yes! This is
Finally me!

8
Grateful Thanks

Oh how I feel so 'blessed' to be
Able to write, to paint
To receive 'inspiration' when my
Mind becomes quiet... to tune in
With a greener shade of security, with
Friendship.

For that light, that power of love
Is within 'all matter of things'
As well as human kind.
Even animals sense the greatness
With the creator!
As well as abundant flowers that
Bloom. Helping to keep life smiling!

But sometimes selfish people hurry and
Scurry to be here, to be there?
Can't spare a minute's thought
To become tranquil...

For I believe that starving people
Of this earth who haven't our
Freedom of mind and plenty!
Choose to 'pray' naturally
For those simple things of life
For their hearts and soul are
Ever grateful!
Ever humble!

9
Sunflower

As we watch the pretty face of a Sunflower!
Its golden petals share its
Flamboyant kisses…
For its many 'seeds' of perfection
Shall one day fall at our feet.

Then 'sowing' of its delicate
Seed shall become plentiful…
Upon our pathway to come
Shining with new roots
New growth
Into another radiant flower!
So utterly grand, so very proud
Spreading its golden wings
Upon our worried brow,

Helping to make us smile!

***

North American Influence
(My name was 'Sunflower' at that time).

10
Blue upon the Horizon

Blue upon the horizon…
Yellow daffodil within our hand
We're looking at a beautiful green land
Where the tallest tree touches the
Peaceful sky!

Bird on the wing, just dancing…
Amongst whitest cloud
Helps us feel spiritual, so proud
So we have a need to sing out loud!
Thanking God in prayer.

Hands clasped together; symbolising
Colourful butterfly wings
With angels dancing happily!!

1 1
Colour Ambience

Thank you 'Great Spirit'
For reaching out with your
Colour radiance, reminding me
Of untold gifts, just waiting
To become displayed again.

Not just 'ageing' within my
Earthly mind
Only to have become lost!

1 2
Valentine's Day

I bought myself pretty flowers
And 'I' signed a Valentine card;
For this day, 'I' felt so lonely…
So I shake free love given by
Trees, especially flower buds!

Even those grasses seem to sing!
For when I sit amongst nature
The creator doesn't let us
Down, as white daisy chains become
'Woven' within my hair.

For the presence of loved ones
In spirit, took time with care
Helping to make my day.

Until new clouds might bring 'change'
With 'abundant' roses giving
With comfort.
To remind 'others' like me…

That we are worth loving, to wait
For that golden key, to 'unlock'
Those heavy gates… locking
'Us' in… suffocating.

For so soon that awaited jewellery,
Box shall one day 'shine' its
True worth with extra happiness
Yet to become ours.

1 3
Why Do We Have To Dream?

Why does it seem that some of us
Have to dream?
Why can't we keep loving things
To stay ours?
Without having to give them up?

Why o' why can't a certain happiness
Come towards us freely
So we might 'allow' warmth with joy
To stay closer to our heart; to
Savour! Precious moments that so
Many take for granted?

So that we might learn to smile!
A little more with those simpler
Things of life.
Not to be cast away…
As if our soul doesn't count
Within life's journey.

***

I used to get told off at school for not smiling!

14
Love to Become Freely Ours?

Why does love, faileth me within this life?
Am I ever to become 'A happy man's wife'!
To have the need to love, to share, with honesty?
For just as a flower needs
That caring soul, to belong?

So we need that kind of soul
To grow with our roots
Taking away our earthly pain, that
We sometimes 'share' alone.

For we 'pray' with our faith…
For love's colour… to one day
Shine forth towards us…
Not to have to wait until we;
Are within those heavenly realms!
For true sincerity, with a loving heart
To become freely ours!

15
Daffodil Yellow

Daffodil yellow, kissed my eyes awake this morning…
O' how that painted a delayed smile upon my face,
Taking away opaque moments of yesterday…
So new sun, new cloud, can confirm delayed happiness…
Yet to begin again!

16
Muddy Ground – Then Sunshine!

Sun reflecting on muddy ground
Reminds us of happier times, but
Clouds of sadness still 'return' within
The background.

But for today we need to 'dwell'
On those positive things of life!
For even though we might not remember
Being pushed happily on a swing!
Running through those long grasses
Being chased by family – brothers or sisters.

Spiritual awareness sent out new light
New thinking
When 'our faith' became that stronger
Especially if we already believed
That it's with 'courage' that pushes
Us on… within the big world!
That can become so daunting and
Frightening on our own.

We started talking to flowers and nature,
That got us by; our dreams were with that sky!
Until true reality came in the way of
Writing; or with colour, taking away
Our pain! Then beautiful colours
Of butterflies danced with joy on to
Our paper, or left with a memory upon our mind!

17
Heart on Our Sleeve

I wished I'd have known you better
Before I fell for those eyes with charm
For many of us feel lonely, we
Think we might link on your arm.
Our days were already numbered, but
We couldn't see
We were only thinking with our heart and
Emotions, not our mind.

Yes, we have received that hurt!
Again, it seemed heavier than before
As we found it so painful to say
A definite goodbye.

For 'we' did really love our partners
This new experience should lead
Us to progression
If we don't wear our heart on our
Sleeve next time around.

So we must take things slower, as a
More positive sign becomes a must!
For we all need that warming love
With caring arms.

So we can eventually smile with
Full trust!

18
Swaying Daffodil

Let us ponder with blue skies;
To 'wander' amongst...
Freedom of swaying daffodil
Taking away undue worry and its perplexities...

19
Rain, Then Positive Ray!

Ending of another day
When time was spent on wondering
Where did that sun go?
Tiny birds happy, still chirping from
Tree to tree;
Even singing their favourite tune!

Daffodils waiting in 'abeyance' for they
Need their drooping petals to reach
Forwarding skies…
No sign of brighter clouds; no touch
Of azure blue!

We shall have to wait for an awakening
Moment with cuckoo call…
Encouraging new growth, new friendships.

Encountering many a new day; painted
With positive ray.

20
Early Spring

Spring has come early…
New blossom has begun
Birds singing merry with the new season
New courses to run…
Blue sky beyond my window
Golden light shining through…

O' these wonderful moments
Become 'shared' with beckoning love?
Branches swaying, dancing with
Happier times yet to come!

O' how we 'owe' the creator
Many thank you's…

And may many words rhyme with verse
Within our seasonal spring!

21
Smiling... Yet Still With Pain

Most of us just smile
To hide away our pain
Most of us say yes I'm OK!
Until clouds take it away
With oncoming rain…

So instead of an umbrella, we
Might hibernate instead within the
Shadow of safety within our
Home; behind closed doors.

Maybe our minds, needing still
To roam… find 'cause' for
Our mental pain?

Then maybe our genuine smile
May 'once' again share…

With a 'new gain' of sunshine, flowers
And a beautiful rainbow.

22
Simple Things of Life

Keep your light in your heart and
Keep your soul free…
Walk towards the sunshine and
Know that 'God' is with thee.

Keep your head held high. To those
Mountain tops above, see the
Snow melting, with the 'warmth of His love!'

'Embrace' all 'His power' that is
Always passing you by… then
Say a big thank you not, for
The sake of speaking…
For 'He' will know why.

For beauty is in all life – a glance…
And in a touch… and stay
Forever grateful for those simple
Things of life!

23
Frustrated but Creative?

Feeling trapped within a body
That only 'moves' very slowly…
Can become quite frustrating
So annoying…
But when my writing or painting
Starts to 'dance' within my hand;
Within our minds.

A reminder that life with creativity
Can become kinder
Than with a new day dawning…
Angel wing with spirit
Give unto 'us' unending
Innocent love – within our being!

24
Dreams into Reality

Relaxing within our cars;
Window wound down
We ponder at the beautiful view, with
Wonder, with amazement,
At the creator's skill – His plan.

And as 'we' rethink into our lonely
Lives, instead of the rain
Our ventures need to 'link' toward
New seasons and friendships.

Spelling out 'new hope' with arched
Rainbow chasing… brighter spectrum
With its security, comforting within
Our long lost dreams.

25
Peace be Unto You...

If I had one wish, do you know what it would be?
I would wave a wand over this mad
Mad world to try and make 'one' see...
New white icing I would spread
Just as I would a cake
Try to clean up all the harm
Done for God and His children's' sake.

God gave unto to 'His' untouched
World; to test what our free will would do
'He' gave unto his love and His
Trust and said "peace be unto you."

But as time went by; 'His beauty' was
Still not enough!
Some men ask for wars, and plenty
Of material worth would still not
Fill his trough!

While sweet children of other countries
Are dying of hunger and loss;
They might suffer! But not in
Vain – as they know they will be 'united'
With their cross.

Their simplicity for living, as gratitude
Still comes from within their hearts
'They' shall have earned their freedom
In another life... then 'their free
Will' has to restart.

Time may change our way of thinking
If we are not yet blown away,
Then there shall be that
Empty hole at the end of a perfect day
Then all God's fine creation would
Have to be rebuilt again...

Then God and his simple people will
Speak "Peace be unto you" and
A 'new beginning' shall be left
To reign.

***

North American Indian Guide: 'White Feather'

26
The Daffodil of Love

Stand tall, stand 'proud'
Allow yourself to feel needed again
For 'spirits' love you within your
Pain, within life's strength.

'They' encourage you to smile, so
Stay happy!

For life is good, to become enjoyed
So hold onto nature's finer
Creation within your troubled
Mind, within both hands.

For 'spirit' is within everything
That moves…
As we are all part of this universe.

So you see!

You are all special
Allow yourself to breathe love.
Just as the golden daffodil
Dances with morning breeze.

***

My mum spirit close this day, she loved daffodils

27
Yellow Butterfly

Yellow butterfly
Just touched my arm like a
Small buttercup,
And as I 'cupped' my hand to
Touch it… it seemed to sit a while…
Encouraging my own heart to dance
Sharing its moment; with healing colour
Debonair quality!
And with that 'hint' of worthiness.

***

After an operation

2 8
Why Bother!

You were within my thoughts and
Heart every day
Until now, with the new spring
I didn't know what might become of us?

I only asked for a few days'
Grace, with new space for
Different thoughts, (within my
Own thoughts) with my own
Beating heart.

Just to be 'me again'!

For you wrapped me up within
Your own insecurities; your own,
Fears
'Towards' the future…
So I didn't feel like bothering anymore?

***

Telling it as it is!

29
Why Do Some Mourners Need to Wear Black?

Why do some mourners need to wear black?
It won't bring your loved ones back
If mourners need to weep, and to forever hold on
Opportunity for spiritual growth
Will soon appear as gone.

One should never think of 'souls'
As 'lost' but to learn that
'They' are always there…
Then thank the good Lord for letting
Them pass your way and a true
Happiness comes with care!

There should come a need to wear
Something bright, to lighten up your eyes…
Then rays of new life with laughter
Will show on your face, as well
As you noticing the skies.

Widows and widowers should be able
To accept 'new colours' and 'allow'
A 'new thinking' to rule the day!
As shutting out new friends will
Not just appear as an end!
But grey skies with sad times only
Shall be upon you!

Then the chance of your loved ones'
Spirit being set free
Can rest upon what it is in your heart
And what 'those mourners'' thoughts send…

30
True Love Can Leave Sorrow

True love hidden within our heart
'Vibrates' only with sorrow
For 'one' isn't allowed to 'express'
As that 'opening flower' within the
Garden of your soul...
For when 'you' first met; sacred
Sunset 'shared' with reverence
Until dark shadows took away
That glimpse of heaven!
Only a prickly stem with dried leaves
Became 'left' within the palm of your hand.

All you need now is to blow away,
Those precious moments within
'Beautiful kisses' of yesterday.

Then a new echo shall start to
'Beat' towards the realisation of
Newer found dreams
For new love shall pass
Your way again...
To 'vibrate' with 'beauty' once more.

Holding truth with passion
Without emotional or deep soul pain.

31
Your Corner

Do not allow your heart to become troubled
Allow new clouds with new birds'
Wing to 'share' their flight
Of fancy with your own.

For your own love for life
Should never fail you, only
Allow that freedom
Within your own corner of this world.

32
Comfort or To Hurt?

Night was young, but your face looked pale
Was your heart still 'ailing' for
Lost love or were certain words
Needed to comfort or to hurt?

I did not want to listen to heavy
Mundane chatter…
I would rather hear a toll bell
Tolling. Peering up to greying skies.

Until grey changes into blue then
Sun kissed leaves burning red
Shall sing in harmony, strengthening
My moral within 'vacant' space
Of this sad evening…

Until 'bird calls' beckoned me
To look toward the sunrise of tomorrow!

When new positive thoughts shall
Become more likely with the
Dew of the day!

For my heart so needs solace
Not hurtful love!

***

My own experience

33
Love!

How can love hold strong? If it
Becomes crushed… as that
Withering flower?
How can love become 'sustained'; if
Its petals come away – one by one!

For a 'broken heart' can't mend with
Broken words
As 'passionate kisses' have to
Stay forgotten
Within sacred dreams!

For 'true love' it seems;
Always touches pain
Then 'one' has that 'full price' to pay!

***

After a sad film

34
Stay Patient, Hold On

As we look lovingly at the azure sky!
Morning cloud reminds us
That our own sad heart is
Still beating.

For the shadow of the sun, still 'shines'
Through…

Reminding us that 'we are never
Alone; to stay patient, to hold on!

For love is ever printed within
Nature and within you!

***

Quakers, with their silence, taught me patience

35
Sadness – Then Joy!

Out of deep sadness
Can come joy!
For your tears can change into
Fine rain from heaven! Then 'wiped
Away' from your eyes – cleansing
Unhappiness away…

'Healing sun' shall brighten up your smile!
Many colours of the rainbow shall paint…
Those beautiful flowers!
Lightening and inspiring your day.

36
Never Too Late

It's never too late to mend that broken heart,
It's never too late to say sorry!

Then a warm embrace can welcome
Beloved flowers sharing their
Sweetness, their kisses...

Birds twittering... can greet you
With another new sunrise!

Making way for you both to
Share the new carpet of white
Fresh daisies.

As your hands are 'clasped'
Tightly, innocently, so
Trusting 'together'.

***

My own experience

3 7
Wishing!

We are so wishing for that new soul to
Show kindness, willing to listen!
For us to laugh out loud; to take
Someone's hand, to take away our mask,
To help take away 'life's burden' with
Sorrow; as we have tried so far to grow
And manage on our own.

For with nights so dark, only mornings
Lighten our day! With many birds
Singing, getting us out of bed;
Encouraging our mind to stay happy
Until a 'grey cloud' hovers... when
We find it hard to 'notice' God's
Nature with a smile!
But we do realise that 'courage'
Within; lightens up our earthly lamp again
Letting us know that we shouldn't feel afraid
For God's hand is always there! Reminding
Us that we should stay happy, ever
Beautiful within his garden upon
This earth! That is why we should
Become awe inspired – when sadness
Arises! To be able to 'reach' higher towards an
Aspiring melody... that others can't always hear!

3 8
Helter Skelter!

Another day with happiness, another
Day of sorrow…
It's like being on that
Helter skelter, high up, touching
Pretty blue.

Sun ray so pleased to see us
My own heart still afraid for
Discovery of a happiness at last!
Then negative thoughts point within both minds!

Then instead of 'logic' to help
Us work it out…
We seem to go down fast!
With grey clouds that can only
Give negativity! Although 'we'
Know 'they' can't govern our lives?

For that's why we are given 'free
Will' to learn, to discover
Who we really are?
Today's moments – you don't
Like me – and I do not like you!
So sunset shall become 'painted'
With 'a goodbye' for a while, or maybe…
Forever!

39
Spiritual Awareness

Spiritual awareness is letting 'your
Light' show through...
Bring your fears and hate to
The surface, become a new you!

Give out your hand, it will be taken
Give out your heart, it won't be broken.

Say a prayer now and then
Perhaps for a stranger; even
If you whisper!
Your words never go unspoken!

In the quietness around you, you
Will feel a warm glow!
It might be night, it might be day;
It is like finding good fortune along the way.

You notice that the sunshine
Gives out that extra hue with ray;
The perfect sky becomes so
Much bluer, until the end of day.

Flowers are forever, blooming, trees
Are ever so high!
Butterflies and birds are singing!
And trailing goodwill messages
All over the sky with a theme
Called 'nature'.

O' life can be so wonderful, it is,
There to hold in our grasp
Believe and learn to live
Honestly, then we can take
Away our mask.!

There will be no more sorrow
There will be no more wars
With God and 'spiritual awareness'
We can make our tomorrows last!

***

2nd poem in my 1st published book 1984/5
Inspirational Moments With Spirit

40
So Sad on My Own

Sweet song of youth
Never ever leave me
For I so 'need' your childlike smile
To take away...
'Throbbing pain' left from a
Broken heart!
Left with despair!

For if your full trust was to vanish
Within this 'sorrowful phase'
My 'life' would 'appear' so empty
So barren
Not worth my while, chasing rainbows
Within a new chapter of spring!

That could 'colour' the 'promise';
Of 'new friendships' instead of rain!
Within seasons, that can only move slowly on...

41
You are met with Spirit

Roses within heaven
Are always sweeter?

Just as birds sing their tune, much the merrier!
The sun shines with gold of much richness
Warming towards children and your own spirit!

Our animals are always included
Everything that 'pulsates' within
Spirit seems to still stay free!

There are schools with works of
Art, including play areas within
Magnificent gardens, hospitals,
Libraries.

'Trees' speak with clouds that move,
Echoing much 'enchantment' for
Everyone to hear, to see!

For there is so much quiet with
Rest, for those who need it?

As 'each soul' becomes met with
Greetings, and always with the
'Greatest of respect'.

42
Bird Call

'No' reason to feel sad
When bird call wakes us!
For they sing towards our sleeping heart;
They sound so happy within the background…
Gives us encouragement to get early out of bed.

To open our front door or back;
To greet the morning bird with bread or cake
For 'they' might have little ones to feed?

For we receive pleasure by filling
Our time with this task!
Morning becomes more of a delight!

Then we might say:
Hello sun!
Thank you for lighting up
Our beautiful day again!

43
A Nobody

I didn't really have any name: I was
Just a human being: 'a nomad'
I walked amongst God's hills, amongst
God's clouds… I would disappear
Under his shadow wearing a dark hooded robe
I was a nobody!
I am not a 'negative spirit' but here
To 'help' others, upon this earth,
I give out 'colours' to blend with sun ray!

"I give out only love; to those of you
Who are sad."

I am more 'alive' now
More respected?
Living with an 'angel theme' within
God's given light!

***

(Wrote this before someone's illness)

Monk Influence!

44
Do We Belong?

Our days seem long…
   When we think we don't belong?
Our minds full of emptiness…
   Our bodies might become weak
For love 'we' only seek!
   Then 'we' might ask?
Who is there to trust?
   When honesty becomes a must!
And only the warmth of an animal;
   The strength of that tree,
The almighty sea;
   Encourages us to draw on their smile!
Of inner faith
   Giving us deeper happiness with confidence.

45
New Dew of Sunrise

In torn shadows of the night – look forward
To the coming new day with the new dew
Of morning sunrise!
For then a 'golden ray' can 'kiss'
Many a smile upon your face…

Then all life's avenues, shall 'awaken'
With the new coming of 'spring'
For daffodils to 'sweep' your
Worries away!

46
I'm Still Here

I'm here up 'high' above the mountain
I'm here 'mingled' within God's sky!
I'm here 'echoing' my love to you
I'm watching from above
I'm sending 'you' a dove of peace.

Allowing your 'heart' to become released…
To make 'you' happy
To make you feel free!

All you have to do
Is send 'up' your tears
With your benevolent love
Towards me…
Within the light of heaven!

***

'Male' in spirit to his lady upon earth.

47
Tsunami

Tsunami
Came to visit – taking our lives away!
Our homes!
Our children!
Everything gone…
Cars, houses, people – just fell
Through a big gap
Nowhere solid for 'us' to go…
We are God's children
All the earth 'moved' beneath us
Shifting us along… sucking our
Lives away
But 'our spirit' held strong!
For our souls are good
We are not 'responsible' for those who fear!
Because others chose to do wrong?*
But we know the 'good' go free!
And live on…

***

Japanese Influence (female)

48
Nature's Own Accord

I came out of my home this morning
Greeting the daily sun!
That helps to take away the dark
Shadow of yesterday…
Thinking of Japan – earthquake
Tsunami with terror!

There to my side new yellow daffodils
Are leaning over, as if to 'weep'
With deep sadness?
Instead of their usual golden joy!
Then I 'notice' a small white,
Daisy! That has just broken through…
Tips of tall grasses were smiling!
As a child of that time was
So grateful to have 'clung' onto life.

We guess it wasn't 'her time' to
Become 'swept' away by 'cruel seas'
Or to have become 'sucked in'
Through Earth's crust… that
Decidedly 'broke up' with nature's own accord…

My own day came 'spent' with the fairer
Land of England!
Marvelling with 'newer joy' of a blossom
Pink tree that 'appeared' more
Colourful with pride. In memory of the
Japanese faithful… who had to
'Bow' their heads… towards their
Maker and towards their new life!
Japanese influence!

49
Faith

We hold onto strength as 'that' hidden
Within a rock!
We are those 'sheep'
Bleating within a flock!
We are those colours portrayed
Within each flower!

So we should hold onto 'faith'
Every second, minute or hour
For we might 'need' to ask
For God's help for 'healing'
Mental or physical pain!

Then 'we' need to 'seek' towards
'Inner truths…' helping 'us' to
Stay courageous and sane!
So please, 'faith', don't ever go away…
For your 'beauty' would not
Glisten! Anymore
For earthly mist would 'shade'
Our own hidden 'loveliness'
Leaving only 'darkness' upon
Our pathway!

50
For the Love of an Animal

I care for my little cat, as I would
Tend to a child
She sits on my lap, licks my cheek
She is so gentle and so mild
She speaks to me with her caring
Eyes, that says she is happy
In our home
Whenever I am ill, she lies on my
Lap so quiet
She never wants to roam…

The rewards one can get from an
Animal, can teach us many truths
We might want to delay.
As our 'vibes' can reflect a fear,
Or harmony and 'they' will let
Us know by coming near, or simply
Running away…

You might have to 'earn' that trust
In a small bird, you might say; 'absurd'
But with tolerance and patience on your side
A 'knowing' will tell you that you
Have become a better person and
That you have finally thrown away that pride.

As an animal came into your life
For a reason, as that is God's way
You might look up to the sky and
Wonder why?

The 'answer' comes with the person
That you have now become; and
By putting a 'love' in your olden ways.

***

Husky my cat, 'she' was 'a leopard' I knew in a past life
(1 of 3 cats)

23rd April 1983
Inspired to write

51
A Glance, a Touch

Just a glance!
Just a touch!
   Conveys so much,
No need to speak, I feel a-blush
At my cheek!
   My eyes seem to smile!
I sense beauty…
   Too delicate to grasp!
The spell might break! Such
Pain would leave me as before…
Within a tangled web; not knowing
What 'life' has to offer?

For you gave unto me; aroma
Of red roses, allowing me to feel secure,
Please say that this is how it shall
Always be?

Just 'place' your heart next to mine
For then I might receive an answer.

For today… might stay; as if
I have the whole world at
My feet… tomorrow may become
Empty! Then shower 'me' with
Petals, not of sweet roses…
But of sweet, sweet, sorrow.

***

Spirit influence (1800-19th century)

52
Who is that Looking at Me

Behind your own eyes; what do you see?
You noticed 'your' reflection and
Asked 'who is that looking at me?'
With bated breath, you wonder why?
The question never 'appeared' within
Those years that rolled by…

Lines upon your face show 'memory'
Of laughter and pain for only sadness
Covers your mirror
Fears for the future remain!

Your life was once fancy free
Now 'you' learn that this 'new
Age' and 'your age' do not agree?

Oh how you need to settle down…
Or 'one' might 'appear' selfish
And alone!

You need someone to find 'hidden
Sensitivity' within your heart, then
Encourage you to make a happy
Laughing home.

For if it becomes too late… that
Family tree will not come your way…

And passed to spirit as 'a bachelor'
Shall be all your earthly epitaph
Shall say…

53
Freeing Emotions

Open up saddened eyes
To beauty all around
For there is so much 'solace'
To become found.

When 'one' becomes so still... then
Stillness can remind you of
Music stirring...

Your inner ear can hear bird
Wings flapping...
Leaves flowing towards the ground
Sacred moments can become shared
Upon sacred earth.

Touching sensitive feet, pulsating
With our sacred emotions
That had become 'hidden' and
Not free!

54
Love is Still Good

Allow 'evening shadow' to wash upon your hair
For 'your love' is still as great
To me – as it was when 'we' were young!
For we never grew old when
'We' linked with 'spiritual' young love!

For your eyes shall always 'stay'
Cheerful and carefree...
For 'our' hearts shall always
Remain 'linked as one'!
Just like a flower, reaching towards the sun!

Wonderful moments' growth shall
Always stay a part...
I ask that my smile with prayer
Shall 'ever' print 'my love' and with
High regard to you...!

***

From a stranger to a lady upon the earth

55

From Your Eyes

From your eyes came many
Colours – some of mauve, some of blue!
Allowing 'us' to realise that
You were filled with kindness
And with humbleness so true!
Your pink cheeks gave way to many a smile,
That spoke of wisdom with trust,
For your spirit gave out much
Joy with happiness.

Even birds and animals 'shared' time
Within your care
Many a time 'you' stood at your
Gate… adoringly looking at your
Hollyhocks and pink roses…

Allowing little children to 'tug' at
Your apron pocket… to discover
That hidden sweet protected
Within a wrapper!
Anything they had to say, 'you'
Noticed their sadness or their hidden
Talent of every living soul… even
A dragonfly… was
Meant to touch upon this earth
To discover the beauty of
Cherry blossom, forget-me-not flowers
Or a poppy!

***

Helga influence

71

56
Blossom Pink

Carpet of 'sweet blossom' pink upon the ground...
Like long lost treasure being found
Birds winging within branches singing
Resonating with a new theme!

Then need comes to us, to 'spread' our
Own wings too
For 'within quietness' we discover what
Is really true!
As we sense 'God' is at hand
For 'He' so created these lands,
Flowers amongst grass with a sense of
Freedom for us to take pleasure!
Within nature's treasures, always to
Become found, when our earthly
Eyes become 'opened', when we look!
On... to discover with a magnificent
Blossom tree for free!

Then for us to walk hand in hand
As brother and sister!

***

Monk influence

57
I Sense your Smile!

As I 'see' a flash of colour that is 'kindled'
Within a flame!
I 'sense' your smile upon your face, then
The smoke 'spells' out your name
I know 'you' never left me; some day
My time will come...
Joining you over the threshold
Then 'our' souls shall become as one!

But at this moment in time, our memories
Of sweetness shall never fade...
You touch my shoulder with warmth
Covering me as a cloak.

Then 'your spirit' returns again towards
Those higher spheres...
As I know that is where
'You' must be?

You send out a cool breeze, that
'Blows out' my candle; but my
'Earthly eyes' can still see!

Perfumed lavender 'entwines' around my
Weakened body, allowing me to know
That 'you' are still there?

For 'eave of silver kisses' – fly free
Upon the air! Quiet laughter humbly
'Speaks' of our own true love
We know is so very, very rare!

58
Sharing Pain

I share your smile
Your pain!
Your dreams like flamboyant sails
Needing to reach the 'sanity of land!'
Where shadows of footsteps can
Become 'heard' yet again!

Then open songs 'vibrate' with seagulls of the sky!

Reminding 'us' why we're here
Within a challenging space of 'deep'
Sorrow or extra happiness!

59
Child Sitting on the Lonely Step

Gives me tears, makes me weep, when
I see a child sitting alone on
Their favourite step or wandering
Alone in their street…

That child appears so lonely, cold
In the rain, maybe not wanted at home!

No loving arms, no one to ask 'where have you been?'
Door key tucked in the pocket
(Known as the latch door kid).

Maybe a few pennies to 'tide' you
Over, a toffee apple or that
Bickie, giving that food comfort.

Better shut the front door, neighbours
Naughty kids with water pistols
Aimed through the clicking letter box!

Shouting 'Old Mother Riley are you
Coming out! We want to play
With your crutches, hobble down
The street!'

To get away from bullying or muddled
Thoughts, I would 'sit' amongst
Nature's flowers, tall trees growing
So very high!
'They' got me through…?

I used to say hello to those birds
The colourful butterfly
'They' whispering your beliefs are true!

As communication with 'creation' was
All the 'trust' I understood…
Even black sky moon, shining with
Stars 'echoed' their music
Encouraging my lonely heart to smile!

Started to sketch, matching words into song
Then my tears could fall free!

So when I watch that lonesome
Figure sitting upon their favourite step!

My past often 'repeats' back to me
At least now, I have that
Choice, I have a voice?

Many 'blessings' I prefer to share…
Allowing people to know that
I understand, and that I shall always care!

***

My own life experience

From a dream with a Victorian link, of a boy sitting on a doorstep

6 0
Positivity

Oh little band of secrets…
What is to become of me?

Might I become a 'true writer'
With paintings set within many frames?

Then positive stronger expectancy
Shall help me come away from just dreaming!

For child's pain has 'taught' me
Many things… leaving 'wisdom' or
Character within daily frown!

Even broken lined pavement, became scary?
Bringing an 'unhappy' omen?
If I went against the grain
That would leave me with
Negative thoughts, I guess forever!

***

My own experience from a child into the eighties.

61
Life Isn't Such a Burden

Although 'we' might experience mental
Or physical pain
We can still 'learn' to give! Share
A smile… with strangers, to
Help 'paint' colours within their day.
Then 'inner pain' within 'oneself'
May 'touch' upon that rainbow,
Giving 'you' a healing!
Then life might not seem such a burden
But a good reason for living…

62
Be Yourself

Within night shadows your heart shall
Be in need of me
Your thoughts might spin and twirl,
Getting out of control…
Start to feel sorry for yourself! Still
Linking to the past?
So new ideas might never, ever be!
For you 'choose' to stick to the
Way it was…
Not!
Thinking or linking, to how life should
Really be, within 'modern ties' of
True reality!
To start to 'express' who 'you' really
Are; or to speak with more vocabulary
And not! To give in to
Mimic anymore!

63
Newness

A baby's cry... a new earthy soul;
A new bud... becomes a new flower!
A bird's chirp... gives out a new song!
A golden dawn... a new beginning
A new understanding... a different me!

***

North American Indian influence

64
Free to Dance

I need to quench my thirst
And wipe by brow!
Echo out loud…
Just let me be!
For I need to become free… on
This hot sunny day

For my emotional pain to be taken
Away by 'flying pollen' irritating
With butterfly frivolity!
So I may borrow, primrose
Smile, then to dance a while…
With melody of peaceful heart!

65
Love within a Star

Our lives with love, seem so far far away…
But 'shines' with the radiance of a star!
Shall it ever have need to
Reach towards us… to help 'free'
Our binding pain?

Then new love, with compassion, might
At last 'unite' within our lives!

That so many 'choose' to take
For granted?

6 6
Words

Words with vocabulary must never
Be 'allowed' to pass us by…
For 'they' shall become lost!
Become hidden within the sky!

Many patterned clouds, need to become
Caught, then sought out…

Then allow 'them' to dance into
Verse or poetry
For 'words' can help people in
Need, small or stout!

'Words' should stay kind with honesty,
As music to the inner ear!

I ask that my mind shall always
Stay 'open'… and for my 'guided
Pen' to stay loyal within my hand.

Encouraging spiritual patterns with
Truths onto paper…

Always creating…
Always smiling!
Always happy!!

67
Hidden Seed

Just as a seed becomes 'hidden'
Within a flower!
So that precious seed becomes
'Hidden' within each one of us?

Just waiting to be set free...
Then to bloom!
To colour!
Then for us to experience
Delayed happiness;
Delayed expression!

68
Row of Pearls

One row of pearls
Became 'shown' to me within a dream
I awoke startled!
Began to wonder what could it mean?

Am I going to win some luck?
Might 'they' become 'found' within
Some forgotten treasure
Or are 'they' symbols of tears?

Reminding me of anxiety and fears…
With memories of past years!

Then beautiful pearls start to 'shine'
With sway…
Sending melodious new hope 'towards'
Our day…

Maybe 'we' have to wait for
That 'new element' with
Surprise, or with bafflement?

Bringing sunshine 'wrapped' around
Those wishes?
That might now come to
Fruition? Proof! Towards
Myself and to you?

***

69
Madness and Stability

Dancing and prancing within weathered storm
Does not 'appear' the norm!
Unless 'madness' takes over from sensibility?
Deadened voice needs to scream!
To challenge thunder
That goes bang!
Until lightning flashes – becomes your
Friend for a while!
It's like dangling and hoping to
Stay alive on a delicate spider's web!
Until big horrible reality hits you
Where 'you' might fall into 'oblivion'!
Until darker shadows 'lighten' again
Within a new patterned sky!

Then 'you' become 'free' to wander,
Within free lullaby!
Where your God might 'touch' your face…
Echoing that all is well
All is forgiven!
Encouraging your soul to 'dance'
Awhile with normality...
That only 'some' may choose to understand!

7 0
Alfredo in Rome

My heart went out to 'Alfredo', I'm
Sure I was not alone.
'He' trod amongst the grassland
Didn't see the 'well' beneath the hole!

Sad darkness that surrounded him
'He' must have felt so afraid!
But we know angels of God were
With him giving some strength
Throughout the day.

Mud and earth were tight around
Him, if only he could see some light?

He thought his mother and papa had
Left him, but we knew of their awful plight!

All attempts to 'free' him, drilling
Through rock and core... 'Alfredo'
Felt tired, closed his eyes and
Slipped a little bit more...

Peace at last was with him, 'He' now
Has spirit children as friends.
Angels and beauty now surround him, shall
Help to make amends.

Flowers I picked for my little church
Was to say 'we cared'.

Yellow for 'Alfredo', for brightness I'm
Sure 'He' always shared...
Mauve was for healing, that will
Be needed for his parents in Rome!

Like the harvest needs blue sky and
Sunshine!
They shall never walk alone!

God bless them!

(True Story)

71
Sarah

While you rest and sleep my darling
The angels of heaven are with you!
Giving you 'the kisses' that we all send dearly
Our little princess, we are
So missing you, our little one
But your smile shall always
Remain within our hearts.
For we know that 'your spirit'
Shall always be there for your
Brother and sisters;
Your lovely mummy and daddy.
'Your spirit' shall 'always' be there
To play with them!

And as we 'look' up to earthly sky!
Your prettiest eyes shall ever
'Dance' with beautiful colour and sweetness…
Our little Sarah, forever 'our princess' child.
Never, ever to become forgotten!

72
Are We Afraid to be Happy?

Are we afraid to be happy? To laugh
Out loud, just as others do?
For life is full of complications
Then we might say "why isn't
Life more simple?" To be 'able' to
Accept that 'love' towards us!
Without sensing that hidden hurt, within.
For 'some' we might have experienced
Rejection; or people letting us down?
Promises are not met?
Siblings or parents, even a friend
Doesn't seem to have that sensitivity.

So sometimes we might become 'left'
With a feeling of mistrust, with negativity…
Which doesn't help if 'one' isn't
That strong within their daily thoughts.

So to be laughing out loud naturally,
To be happy, as others around us seem to do;
Is something we have to work
With as 'maturity' comes into play!
Until a realisation allows
Us to say: yes! We are allowed
To be happy, we are 'allowed' to
Feel part of this universe;
With other people and with
Ourselves!

73
Rosemary

Dearest Rosemary, do you remember
'Us' at school?
When you and I used to run
Around… and generally 'Play the
'Fool!'

With Iris and Jean; we were the
Troubled four.
We used to hobble down the stairs
Hiding from the teacher's door!

Dearest Rosemary, you were always
Pale and so weak.
But your spirit held strong – only
Laughter stayed within your heart…
You gave courage for others to
Seek!

'You' would not eat all your dinners;
Oil capsules you would burst under
Your shoe
Milk would be poured down the
WC. Then pretend 'you' had
Taken your vitamins with a straw?

Secretly, I tried to help you eat
Those things you disliked to
Try and make you well!

But 'you' always refused, to treat it
Like a game… as if 'you' knew
Something but could not tell?
Four of us would paint and
Sketch together; with an eagerness
To express creativity.

Funny faces 'you' would make, 'you'
Didn't want to be that true saint?
'You' had beautiful golden locks,
Matching your spring dance!
Your parents must have been
So 'proud' of you – so petite, so bonny
As that living doll!

Your body became very frail. We
Think 'you' knew that heaven
Was soon to come your way…

'They' laid you to sleep with
'Your secret' dolly and
Small teddy bear.

Many fallen tears were shed
For you – dearest Rosemary…
For we all deeply loved you
We shall forever miss your
Happy spirit, what more can we ever
Say!!

***

We went to Cloudesley School, N.I. Rosemary passed to spirit
aged just 14.

74
Can You Play Today?

Little boy can you play out today?
Come and kick your ball about…
Or might your daddy have something to say?
Your innocent eye says all
That needs to be said
For daddy! When in an angry
Mood; that hard spanking might
Put 'you' to bed!

That bottle of coloured water
Is all that 'he' shows within his hand!
He appears such a miserable
Man; yet still thinks he's
The cream of the land.

So stay strong little one
For you've learnt to grow up fast!
So protect your mummy and
'Pray' that this private hell
Might not last!

We shall call for 'you' tomorrow
For the day might 'shine' something
New! So 'paint a smile' across
Your face, knowing it might
Be the only thing left for
You to do!

***

Gives me tears

75
What Does the Future Hold?

As we look yonder to the centre
Of that tree; our inner thoughts
Might be asking…
What does the future hold for me?
As years gone by… the past
Hasn't been so fine – our inner
Thoughts wishing to reach out for
Good health – like the sweetness of wine!

For many flowers with colour, bring
New change into full bloom!
Like noticing those stars within
The black sky… passing the
Stillness of the moon!

Spiritual uplift– we ask for
Ourselves and the world,
Giving strength, support with
Harmony – within our daily lives!
As our hidden roots are now
Opening out… towards truth that
Is now 'surrounding' our warm and winding trail…
For if we 'sow' good seeds… our
Tree shall bear good fruits for all…

Keeping our branches high!
Touching the sunlit sky, making
'Us' feel so very tall"
For if we 'link' to 'our tree daily', it
Shall help 'our lives' a treat!

76
Candle Gives Healing

A candle is loving;
Its brightness takes away 'darkened
Shadows' within the night!
Its warm 'sacred flame' of red, gold
With blue; reminds 'us' of 'yesteryear'
When sadness became the norm!

But now sitting quietly with its new radiance
Allows our own heart to pray, to sing!
As dancing aura reaches as high
As an angel wing!

Until dancing light no longer 'shines' so bright
As natural amber 'foretells' peace
With forgiveness! Giving healing with
Its red and blue!

For ours and your
Past misdemeanours!

***

77
Reflection!

Hold the reflection of loving blue sky
In both hands!
Remember, forever 'all God's' colours
Clothe his 'precious lands'.

Imagine all the skill that has
Become used to make a butterfly wing!
Listen: to the echo of a magical bird song!

Stay ever grateful, for your own
Footsteps, might leave your identity
Upon your pathway…

Always strive to take time with
A friend, and, with the welcoming
Of your warm hand!

78
Twilight

Twilight of sorrow...
Twilight of love!
Twilight of thanksgiving to those 'carers' above!
Mood of joy – mood of contemplation
How significant thou art, to many
Who need to reach beyond reality!
Where 'all' is written within holy light!

Where 'halo of success' becomes....
A challenge to 'those' who are searching!

***

Signor Pierre (French artiste)

Drew a psychic picture at the same time of writing.

79
Forgotten Dreams

Forgotten dreams – O' how I
Remember you well…! When you
Pass my way… you bring me
Back into childlike days, when
I used to be happy at play!

I would skip and dance around a
Merry-go-round… until the night
Drew dark; then at last, I
Closed my eyes… laughter with
Sunshine was still within my heart!

O' forgotten dreams – how I remember you well…
But the past has to be pushed
Aside… then 'renewed' – to allow
Maturity to come into play!

For we must 'bless' our family
And our homes – giving 'opportunity'
To our young
So their forgotten dreams stay
Harmonious and 'laughter' is
Still within their eyes,

So if and when 'they' look back…
To childlike days… there
Shall always be dreams of yesterday
With those new tomorrows…
But never, ever sad goodbyes!

80
My Spirit Dances

My 'spirit' dances, free with a beautiful
Butterfly, as 'one' skims above yellow buttercups…
Helping 'our pain' blow away…
For we mustn't become discouraged
With the grey day just gone by!
But 'allow' music to take away our tears
'Vibrating' good memories, flowing with
Silent breeze!
Just as bird wings need the wind
With a 'spiritual' theme.

So with a prayer of the night;
Golden moon appears bright!
Kissing the ground that 'we' walk upon…
Helping for peace to 'embrace'
All people, with animal kind;
To ever stay 'part' of this
Very beautiful world!

***

81
Your Soul... You Now Have Become

Please accept that I now 'share' a
Place within heaven!
My soul is 'bathed' within God's
Light! Where we are all treated as even?
My spirit is never too far away...
For I am still part of your 'earthly
Times' with your day!

So remember, moments with the centre
Of your favourite flower shall smell
Of your favourite perfume.
You will 'sense' it is me
Fluttering on a sweet butterfly wing;
That soft glow upon a shining
Leaf! Shall encourage your own heart to sing!

So keep forever smiling! Think of
Creation – ever budding – new!
Each new morning sunrise
Shall draw new friendships towards your day!

So never think of yourself as lonely;
For life is far too short to
Think of life like that!
For within 'your school of learning'
Attuning with knowledge shall
Ever 'shine' with growth...
Freely from your own soul! 'Your
Soul' you have now – happily become!

82
Happy Coloured Faces

Happy coloured faces who smile
Within this worried world today,
Keep a strong belief with
Your 'faith' and forever continue to pray?

You might not own much
Within your pocket?
You might be hungry too...

But continue to stay ever thankful!
And, for that innocence inside you!

***

Asian influence

83
Walking Hand-In-Hand

We always liked to walk hand-in-hand
Within parks and close to a fountain
Where innocent children were 'allowed'
To sing amongst green hills that
Could change into a mountain!

We are so lucky to say 'those were
The days…' but still our hearts
Were 'entwined'.
Where nature's hue mingled together
Giving truer meaning within life!
That stays ever young.

The sun so warming, spreads towards
The earth showing 'us' that plant
Or root can ever ripen or grow!
Encouraging 'us' to 'look' to the
Sky; many birds are in flight!
But one fell hard onto the ground! Without a sound!
We cradled him affectionately; buried
His body with great care!
God bless, said we, and may 'peace'
Ever reign… with our hands clasped
Together – light breeze whispered
That 'his spirit' would stay walking
Beside us within our never-ending days.

84
What Kind of Heritage?

What kind of heritage are we leaving our kids today?
By filling the 'atmosphere' not with
Rainbows but with greed and apathy!
Allowing our own selfish desires for material gain
Then becoming 'obsessed' with their ideals
But not as the creator would
Wish them to be?

Compassion from many peoples' hearts
Seems to have blown away...
Then clouds within the sky 'appear'
Sorrowful and grey!

So it's newer attitudes and behaviour
That we all need to seek
To plant new seeds; wiping away
Those wrongs?

Making the way ahead 'clearer' for our children!
Then their children can stay ever united!
Giving reassurance
With a greater need to belong?

85
Smaller Flowers

Oh little flowers
We so love thee...
Forget-me-nots, blue or grey, so precious, so true!
Petite white daisy, waiting to become
Seen, so 'they' may share their
Benevolent smile!

Smaller, scarlet poppy reaches 'our' hearts
With displayed warmth, as it 'kisses' our cheek!

Love with perfume, becomes ours forever?
Including small faced dandelions;
So yellow, so gold!

Swaying amongst tall grasses that
Share happiness, their freedoms!

That can 'lift' our emotions!
If we have experienced; many
'Untruths or painful love'
Within our lives!

86
Dandelion Yellow!

Dandelion of yellow!
Resting upon stem of green
I shall 'always' see 'you' as very beautiful
As some people think that 'you'
Shouldn't be seen?
Even when 'you' open up your 'true
Heart' with the 'glow' of daily sun!
'You' bow your head when it's grey
Cloud with rain!

So when I notice your pretty face…
Humble dandelion…
'You' open up my eyes to bring
That magic within 'my' lonesome day!

***

Helga influence

87
Waiting Welcoming Skies

The sun does shine within moment's song
Then grey cloud moves along the sun's path…
Taking our joy away!

For one moment, a yellow daisy amongst
Yellow grasses, rustic fern
Appears ever smiling.

Then a quick misty shower took away the
Chance of a pretty picture for our album?
We shall have to hold on?
For another day when welcoming
Skies choose to dream with
Our moments.

Enhancing sacredness within the forest…
Within you
Within me!

88

Enter Those Deserts of Eternity

Enter those deserts of eternity
Allow all wrongs of yesteryear...

To change into a fine dust!

So that hate and anger, can blaze free...
Upon the orange flamed fire!

***

Arab link

89
Two Hearts

Why should 'two hearts' seem better than one?
Is it because we are humble and need
An end to loneliness…?

For when we need to cry – a new
Shoulder will be there…?
A happier smile may 'derive' when
Troubles are shared!
Maybe more confident, to make new friends.

On windy, wintery days two souls
Can become entwined! For warmth
With 'love' can take up our time –
Walking together – hand in hand
As two children playing nursery rhymes!

Dancing in two-step – even treading on
One's toes… it does not seem
To matter – as companionship becomes
The greater!

Mundane heavy thoughts… just
Flow away with those grey clouds…

Helping one another, listening
To nature, flowers and trees…
Yet still 'aware' of your own
Heartbeat – always as individuals!

90
My Love for You!

As I give you a bunch of flowers!
The message reads
'I love you'
Their delicate colour and splendour!
Spells out, this is very true...
Inspiration touched with perfume
Are set within stamen so bold!
For within my heart and emotions,
I would display my love
To you – with gold!

***

Victorian link

91
Why Can't We Become the Same?

Everything seems so tranquil when
'We' watch those ducks and swans!
Resting so softly upon those daisies…
So pure – so silent! Amongst
Tender blades of grass mingling
Between – make it all seem so friendly!

My own heart wonders
Why can't we 'all' become the same?
Reminiscing together… allowing our
Own individuality to compromise with sincerity!

Not hiding behind feeble excuses?
As reality must be 'allowed'
To play a part; to show
'Compassion' from our hearts… so
Honesty can 'show' through…

Then our own minds shall 'yearn'
To become free again!

Allowing ourselves to mingle with
Those birds and white daisies!

Feeling happier – more content!

92
War and Peace!

Can we experience peace?
Yes!

If we learn to tolerate each other
And to look at the other side
Of the coin!

To notice that 'full goodness' with
Forgiveness is there within us all!

That we are 'blessed' forever
Walking with beautiful bird kind.
To grow tall amongst tree roots
And be 'proud' to hold that
Hand of another...

Allowing us to 'learn' with those
Memories on past hates with sorrow!
Then with many tears left behind!

Let us be glad to be who 'we'
Are? To help God build that
Earthly bridge.
For us to walk towards
That 'peace'!

And that 'war' shall become as
A symbol of the past!

93
White Dove of Peace!

Think of that white dove of peace!
For this shall bring healing with release…
Release from many stresses;
Insecurities with pain!
Then a 'new ray of light' shall
Be 'able' to re-awaken your
Heart – your mind!
Towards the way you 'appear' to
Others; maybe to start thinking anew!
Within daily life!
And towards daily loving!

***

Quakers gave me peace sitting with their quiet.

94
Shelter of Your Wing

How great thou art!
When 'we' can sit with quietness;
Your solitude…
For under the shelter of your wing!
We are as little sparrows – needing
To become 'nurtured' within 'your
Love' – courage and salvation!

95
Eternal Faith

O' eternal faith, never ever leave us!
Stay upon those branches, displaying
Courage to stop 'us' from falling!
Please speak with 'us' – within the pulse
Of those green leaves, shadowing within
Those waters…
Within the 'shade' of your sky!
Within 'the smile' of your sunflower!
Please keep 'us' within your debt;
So that 'we' may stay ever humble;
To do good unto others. To
Eventually give benefit to all.

96
Caring Heart

Allow a broken heart to 'listen' to long lost music…
So its melody can 'etch' new
Meaning, encouraging newer ideas; with positivity!
For when a caring heart of another,
Has to say goodbye!
New challenges with tomorrow may
Bring younger spectrums amongst
New flowers breathing!
Then benevolent freedom shall help
'Your delayed smile' to return!

As 'repeated memory' shall soon
Fade… 'as caring heart' broke
Away from olden green stem as
'It' wasn't strong within life anymore!

But within the new season – new space, shall
Inspire new messages of pleasure!
With new hope 'hidden' within
Life's mystery.

Not truly forgetting the 'caring heart'
That held much courage –
Within pain?

97
Tides of Fortune

Allow tides of fortune, never to pass you by…
Stay positive with smiles, to lighten up your day!

For life is what we make it, can
Become shaped to ever shine!

So be happy, stay strong!
Then a song shall 'vibrate' from
Your own emotions…

Encouraging you to link with tides anew!

Then!
New growth shall ever stay
Plentiful with 'new humble roots'
That you have finally earned!

***

Philosophy

98
Sweet Song of Youth

Hold out your hand, let me know that
You are still strong – share me a
Smile with your eyes – so that you
Shine 'a miracle' for evermore!

Sweet song of youth, I am ever with
You, when moments get sad!
But you my dearest one, I link
To you from heaven!
We dance with 'little animals' and
Pretty flowers, we sing with children
That have gone on before.

I hold you towards my heart for
Just a short while – for I have
To let you go…
For you grow ever kind within
Earthly times, but I shall be waiting
When the 'time' is right for you to stay…

So keep your lips ever pink – your
Hair shining like the dew – to stay
Ever young.
For we shall meet in secret gardens
Where 'we' can clasp our hands
For evermore!

***

Edwardian link
Gentleman in spirit to his lady love

99
In the Month of May

In the month of May…
I found a new love, although it's
Giving me pain to finally 'let' you go!
But when I look up at those
Roses, I sense your smile giving approval?

Then with 'bird song' came your
Kindness; with new hope for the future, to be.
For 'your' soul left this earth to
Reach toward higher things, your roots
Were re-planted, but you know
That 'your' colour with shade shall
Always stay with me, upon this
Earth plain forever! Within loveliness of
Different 'flowers' and within every season.

***

Writing about Reg, he passed about 1989

100
Don't Allow Deep Sadness...

Don't allow 'deep sadness' to take over
From the joys of spring!
Or let 'it' stop butterflies dancing
Upon your hand or, to close your
Ears to 'hear' a lark sing
For the tender touch of a
Butterfly's wing can send moments of
Glad tidings so soft like velvet.

Do not 'shut out' inspired moments
To 'hear' their tiny footsteps for
'Peace' they might have 'printed' upon you...
So honest, so colourful so true!

Allow purity from their hearts to
Bring a rainbow hue; wiping all your
Sad tears away...

Allowing all birds and the butterfly
'Spray' moments of tenderness
Making your and theirs
A just perfect day.

***

Helga, Victorian

101
A Wood Pigeon

As I watch a pretty wood pigeon
He rests upon my garden tray;
I ask "Dearest pigeon, what news
Have you for me today?"

As my only contact with the 'outside'
World; is looking through net
Curtains that let in some light!

I 'venture' secretly into peoples'
Lives daily while I keep out of sight!

No one knows of my 'solitude'…
And how an urgent need becomes
Inside myself to have some
Idle chatter.

But out there, They are young
And carefree! Their own lives
Is all that seem to matter?

I have shed many a tear within
Those years that have rolled by…

All I have is an old photograph
Of my dear one who was
Killed in the war!
We were not blessed with a son or daughter!
Who would have shared chuckles
With laughter!

My daily homecoming of this pigeon
Is all the 'love' that
I need; as 'He' won't let me down!

'He' swoops from my oak tree…
Then a deep red rosebud
'He' picks up from the ground!
His sweet cooing translates
Into fine music… as he drops
The flower upon my sill…

New reason beckons me to open
My window outside…
Then hidden succour with the
Perfume of life – hits back at me!

A new light softly speaks to me
That my life should become
'Lived' to the full… then
Finally set free!

Then to 'venture' out, maybe
To sit at my gate!
Allowing my own eyes to
'See' with new realisation… that
The world as well as 'ourselves'
Are always loved and ever beautiful!

From an old lady

102
3 Pennies

As I sit under the lamplight, its
Light shines upon my hand!
I have only three lonely pennies…
Instead of golden nuggets; but
To me 'they' still appear as grand!

Three pennies would not buy
Much; but I have more than
Enough within my heart.

I have had a happy marriage
And three children from the start.
They have cried, they have
Laughed… we all have
Had so much fun!

All the gold dust within the
World would not 'match' their
Eyes lighting up with the sun!

They all have grown up now;
My husband is older and sitting
Quietly at home.
But 'we' can take a nap, please
Ourselves; wherever 'we' wish to roam…

Grandchildren 'we' hear in the background
'They' mix with different colour
And creed with manners of spiritual
Worth, is so very much to please!

Animals – 'they' trust with good care
For a certain kind of warming
Love is 'painted' everywhere!

All the money in the land would
Not change my life and my way?
I just prefer to sit 'gazing'
At those three lonely pennies...
And give thanks to the good Lord
Above! And to the ending of
Another beautiful day!

***

Victorian link, wearing a bonnet

My Nan actually spoke these words, to give 3 pennies to
others if they hadn't eaten...

103
Sweet Summer Rose

Why do I remember 'you' as that
Sweet summer rose?
Your heart centre, forever young
And tender!

Your face reminds me of a waterfall…
With much colour to render!
Your eyes are still gleaming!
So soft in splendour!

Calming aroma surrounds your
Pure white skin.
Your cheeks are 'pink' like
Powder puffs!
Showing childlike features within.

Fantasies and fairy-like times we
'Shared' together with all four
Seasons, with new 'buds blooming' forever!
Our dreams never to become broken!

So give me your lily white hand
O' my sweet summer rose
Allowing our hearts to ever entwine…
For 'God' and angels are with
Us, encouraging another new day of time!

***

Victorian 1800's link

104
Different Season

We held hands for a while
My heart began to smile!
But as a 'new season' came upon us,
I knew that you weren't going to stay!

All my dreams seemed to be in vain!

But God's help pushed those grey clouds along…

My thoughts started to 'focus'
With the colour of those prettier flowers!
Fairy-like trees, swayed with 'all
Creativity'.

At last I knew I would be cared
For with humility, security and grace!
Until new friendships may come within that
Different season!

105
Deepest Red Rose

Deepest red rose, clinging to a gate
Reminds me of a 'prisoner' held
Behind iron bars hidden away;
Not knowing what 'his future' might bring?
For as I 'sense' that
'Sweetest love' within 'rose kind' and wonder?
'What love might 'once' have become
'Hidden' within that soul?

Was he 'battered' as a child – maybe
Didn't know 'the meaning of parents'
Only went towards crime
Or stealing; or maybe worse!
Getting… someone's attention
Because 'they' haven't been heard!

For I'm sure that there is some
Good within 'a disruptive soul'
For we are told that 'we' once
Were born into a perfect world…
But now, too much material gain
Reflecting! There is bound to be
Some suffering.

So let us not always 'judge' others
For their failings or misfortunes
But to 'send' a spiritual light
Of 'true worth' towards their hearts…

For them, in time… 'they' might notice
That a loving seed has become
'Planted' with 'them' in mind?
And for once!
That rose tree might 'awaken'
Their own thoughts towards love with
Beauty within.

As well as within themselves!

***

Victorian link (Helga)

29th June 1992 – Finsbury Park
Inspired to write

106
Newer Found Dreams

Under the shade of 'an old oak tree'
'One' can relax; and feel those blessings!

For then 'sun ray' can 'peep' through…
'Kissing' one's cheek!
Helping your heart to know of
That 'warming' at the ending
Of a perfect day!

Then new sunrise shall 'awaken' your
Thoughts with those newer found dreams…!

Waiting, just to become discovered by
You and by me!

Monk Influence

107
Life is a Challenge

Life is a challenge
And should be greeted with new
Expectancy from you!

Then the simplest of hearts can appear
Strong with courage, that shall
'Paint' within torn shadows of negativity!
Allowing new white clouds of dreaming
To dispel those myths;
That only some are the chosen few!

For we are 'all God's' perfect flowers;
And given 'opportunity' to
Grow, to bloom, – abundantly within
'His' colourful garden!

***

Tibetan Monk link

108
Loneliness

Loneliness can become a nightmare if
You allow 'it' to get hold of you;
For all we need is that warm hand
With 'encouragement' for us to plod on through!
But what if we become deeply troubled and
Pessimism is all that we know?

Then 'we' are not helping to get rid
Of the matter – only 'heartache' will
Be 'allowed' to grow!

So when you 'notice' that sun is shining
That was once 'hiding' behind!
A darkened cloud… know that this
Is a gift of a spiritual kind
With 'its' radiance speaking out loud!

Allow 'your soul' to touch its brightness
Allowing your eyes to become
Full of good cheer!
Then you shall 'see' delayed
Kindness within people's hearts.

Then you must be 'prepared' to reach
Halfway, bringing friendship towards
Them – who might be 'lonely' too?
For then you shall start to
Live life to the full!
So happiness instead of 'rejection'
Shall be 'allowed' to
Follow through!

109
What Do We Do?

What do 'we' do within our day?
Do 'we' find time to listen within;
To listen for those birds that
Echo with their song?
Or hopefully 'wait' for that first
Ladybird to enjoy our friendship!
So we can 'marvel' 'all nature's plan' together...

For sun rays we can visualise
'Pictured scenes' within vibrations
Of each petalled flower bud; or
Music dancing with a fallen leaf!

For our material mind can become
As peaceful as morning clouds within
Every day's long...
Helping to make those 'hurried'
Times – so different from the rest!

Then tomorrow you might sigh, not
With tiredness but from 'experiencing'
Something exceptional!
For now you sing with 'new pleasure' –
That holds 'new memory'
That can become kept...
Within your mind so sacred!
For that rainy day!

110
Hearts and Roses

Hearts and roses I give unto
You – expressing a deep message of love!
For every day I give thanks; for
'Allowing' me 'the privilege' of
Knowing who 'you' were!

For your spirit 'shone' so much light;
But now has become my gain!
For within nights I don't feel so lonely any more...
Then with 'morning sun' as well
As 'night star' shining!
It still doesn't seem enough?

Without 'wisdom' – portrayed from
Your own eyes!

***

Edwardian, from a male to his lady in spirit

111
Within Gardens of Love

'Within moments' of peace, within gardens of love!
Sense its 'peace' within your own
Heart; to ever keep you strong!
For if 'life' seems 'grey' and distant...

Pray for sunshine to glow, as if
Morning dew has 'kissed' your cheek!
Then 'within moments'' day long, new
Flowers shall start to bloom!
Shades of many colours with
'Blossoming' courage shall help to
Lift your soul!

***

112
Beautiful Bird Song

Within beautiful bird song
Comes a melody just for you
To brighten up your eyes
To help you smile through.

For the turning of events might have
Upset you – so you forgot to
Look at the joy of the blue sky!

So know and trust that there is hope
Within your new day
That 'bird song' shall ever 'awaken'
Your spirit to ever greet you within,
Those happier summer mornings!

***

113
My Cup Runneth Over...

My cup runneth over, but not
With sweet wine, but with 'tears'
For you – 'dearest one'
You came into my life for such
A short time – you 'passed' through
Without a goodbye!

Awakening dreams allow me to know
It is you by my side
I reach out to touch your
Silky white hair
Then you disappear
Into nothingness… only 'your'
Spirit is there?

O' dearest one, someday I
Shall come unto you – where
Our hearts shall be as one!
To become within 'your world'
Once again!
For to hold 'you' within my
Arms – is but one of my deepest desires!

***

Shakespearean influence

135

114
Frosted White Patterns

Frosted white patterns forming within a blue sky!
Display many pictures within day going by…
Some remind us of snowflakes!
Some very smooth – swept and refined!
Many clouds form into faces or castles
Some as sea waves – painted with
An artist's flair!
Breaking up once saddened thoughts
Allowing a sweet delicate
Butterfly to 'kiss' our tears away…
For behind our darkest day
Silver light is there for
'Us' shining!

Echoing hidden courage
Confirming
That 'our spirit'
Has finally won!

***

Edwardian, 1900's

115
Dancing White Butterflies

Two white butterflies chasing and dancing
Touching tips of grass, that is shining.

Wings touching... small white daisy
Amongst green stems, so proud!

We watch in 'awe' with wonder of
Their perfection with skill!

As their delicate wings 'unite' sad
Memories wishing that 'we'
Could dance again with that new chance!

Especially watching married couples so happy!
Some of us can't remember mum or dad holding hands...

Some of us might reminisce with
'A tear' to 'our eye'!
When we 'link' to mum and
Dad fighting, never laughter for
Siblings to share.

Mum is usually the one that
Has to be strong, to keep
Her family together, maybe wearing
Hand-me-downs.
Encourage us to stay grateful
For small mercies...

Loneliness with fear grew within!

It became so hard to trust!
To 'ask' for help in any way
As family needs to stay intact…

Didn't want to be 'separated' or
To be sent away…

116
Pipe of Peace

As we 'sit' in circles shining yellow
Sun, shine on faces!
Palms of hand 'open' reaching bluer sky!
Our eyes follow 'birds' that fly on the wind...

Grey clouds 'promise' rain to
Thunder on mother earth!
To give us wheat, to fill hungry bellies
Beating of drums – make music
For our heart to forever sing!

In distance... image of yellow
Cloud, 'our master', our teacher!
'He' sits on white horse both
Hold 'power' given by the 'good Lord Almighty'!

We gather in larger circle all
Love flow from higher spirit,
To our spirit!

We smoke 'pipe of peace' all is well!
Rushing of wind... carried all
'Disharmony' away...
To let 'us' dance in old red
Indian country.

Where mountains are there to
'Protect' all the living.

***

'Whitehart' (Semi-trance)

139

117
Sorrow

Let your 'sorrow' stay part of yesterday
Allowing 'new thinking' to bring in
Brightness every minute, every hour!

So new-found worth shall
Awaken your soul;
Within newer skies of tomorrow!

118
Never Halt the Joy of Spring

Never halt the joys of spring!
Never say 'goodbye' to the tide that is turning…
For new found rays shall soon 'blend'
Within a 'new spectrum' of creation!

Then your own life within life can 'reach'
Out towards a comfort similar
To a yellow daisy growing taller!
Touching the golden sun!

***

Edwardian link

119
Search for your Lost Soul

If there is a need to 'search' for your lost soul!
Look in the running water of a flowing stream
Find 'solitude' in the sway of a tree...
Or within hidden love – in heart centre of a flower!
Watch that kindness in the eyes of a small bird
Trust in the strength of that horse!

Hold faith in what 'clouds' bring tomorrow...
For they might 'end' your search of ever feeling lost...

***

North American Indian link

120
One Poppy Just For You

My spirit 'sees' many red poppies within
A field; just 'one' I pick just for you!
To my love upon the Earth plain…
I miss so very much!

For poppies represent much love
With warmth and happiness!

I'm so sorry I am late in giving
You my message of delayed love!

For a bullet from an enemy's gun
Sent 'my soul' further away from you!
I wasn't able to write that last
Letter of hope with good cheer!
Those small 'secret kisses' at
The bottom of its page.

But if you look out of your favourite
Window, you shall 'see' that
White dove of peace!

Bringing you those godly heavenly
Poppies… just for you…!
So place its red petals against
Your sorrowful heart!
For I shall be there to dry your eyes…

My spirit shall be looking over
You, now and forever…! Always.

Whispering with my hello!
Especially within your new mornings
Where 'we' used to sit, within
Our friendly garden of 'endearment'.

***

1940's influence.
A gentleman to his wife during the war!

121
All is Well

All is well my little flower! That
Dances upon the wind!
Your love for life is now 'reaping'
With many gifts, for your troubles
Have been many!

They now fly away as fine dust
From earth, to make into whirlwinds…

They 'all' disappear into red sunset
And 'go down' with 'hot sun'.

Smoothness of life is 'upon' you friend
We gather around 'you' always and forever!

As we await 'new sunrise'
To 'bless' another new day of time!

***

North American Indian influence

145

122
Little Bird

Little bird sits within my hand;
Tells me of living secrets within 'his' eyes.

Flapping of wings!
Tells me he 'indeed' is
My friend... and all is well!

He 'flies' high to freedom of tree top!
Then 'sweet comfort' is given
Unto me, when I know
'He' is safe and sound!
In nest of grasses that 'he' calls home?

***

North American Indian influence
Spoken to me

1 2 3
Star

Song on the wind!

Bird high on treetop skimming blue sky!

Water running free to touch
Red hot land, where all is so dry!

Silver star shine above blue
Mountain to protect all living
Creatures… and souls that
Roam mother earth!

***

North American Indian influence
(As if talking to me)

124
Sitting Under Trees

Sitting under trees… sitting upon the grass!
Is where I 'sense' I must be?
Then a little secret opening
Inside my heart needs to ask!

Where can I find that 'certain
Peace' or rainbow?

Many answers seem to echo within
Hushed moments…

Rustling wild flowers with the golden
Corn, where blue sky meets…

Amongst those hills and the downs!

Then with new breath… an awakening
Allows 'the new me'

For new jewels with luxury can
Match its beauty of my now given crown!

New sunlight upon the horizon!
Waiting to 'nurture' each part of creation!

When 'all nature' redeems itself
Showing much love for 'us' to render.

Magnificent! Divine!
Everything within this universe is free.
If material matters are cast aside…

Then sitting under trees having
'Freedom' to sit upon
Beautiful green grasses!

Becomes as natural as breathing!
Within 'God's' given 'air'.

***

Edwardian link

125
Willow Tree as a Friend

Willow tree, please become a friend to me!
Take me under your shade, allowing
Me to stay – to feel part?
As I am of the human kind, that
Must not dream too long, amongst
Warming earth…
For that is where your roots belong!

Brush 'us' warmly as the cool wind
Blows, allowing your separate leaves
Of identity to reach ours.
Touching our brow, giving a 'calmness'
Allowing 'us' to see that golden
Light shining from the universe…

Then 'spiritual guidance' shall show
The way to a freedom!
For curling leaves; curling tresses
Rest upon cooling grasses!
Lifting up our earthly hearts when
'We' feel heavy? Needing to 'share'
Your secret moments… beside the
Dancing stream!
Then we need to hold onto your
Wispy strong arms of healing green
Never ever to let go!
For we so need to stay as that
Friend to you too!

***

Helga and Monk influence

126
Delayed Peace

Grey mottled cloud, may trouble the worried brow!
Bringing thoughts of darkness.

But you can mentally hold
Onto wings of a 'white dove' carrying
Your heavy load…

Easing your way out of your wilderness…

For a dove of peace carries the 'white
Purity' of healing!

Touching your own heart gently…
With his wisdom, his gold!
That 'speaks' with angels…

Then gratefulness for delayed gifts with blessings!
Shall, spread outward…
Similar to a palm leaf exploring
Towards new spiritual treasures!

With knowledge…
For you to realise that 'delayed
Peace'… was always there for the asking!

***

Chinese influence

127
Embossed in Pure Gold

As I visualise myself 'embossed' in pure gold
It reminds me of 'olden times' with
Unhappiness when life didn't
Appear worth living!

Then a spirit helper with angels told
Me that one day would
Change with a new way of thinking.

Philosophy with wisdom would start
To 'rule' my mind!

So that pure butterflies would 'kiss'
Me upon my cheek!
Touching me with their healing!
Their honour!

Helping my confused mind to rest…

Then opening… as a butterfly wing
Broadening towards a love!
That I was always chasing…
For I 'sensed' that I never
'Deserved' within life!

For this 'gold' with strength of wisdom
Is 'given' as spiritual gifts earned?

For staying so patient through earthly
Pain with frustration!

For 'our soul of progression' shall ever
Share with others, also that
'Their gold' shall ever 'shine' on…
As a guiding light to everyone!

***

Egyptian link

128
God's Fruits are for All

Life can appear 'pleasing' if one
Realises that God's fruits
Are for everyone!

And that the changing season is to
Become 'a sign' for new growth
That 'channels' new thoughts
To spread into day!

Making way for golden sun strength
To push those heavier
Clouds away…

Then realisation of blue sky!
Can become 'painted' by you
And by those who wish
To see it!

***

Chinese link

129
Tree So Weak

Tree so weak; remind us of how we used to be!
Trying to reach 'taller' towards the
Sky! Helping to make us feel stronger!
Then our branches of frailty
Would not break under those stresses of life!

For 'new hope' of baring new
Greener leaves would give us more
Courage to plod on...
Into 'new positive beliefs' and 'hopes'
With a fruitful future!
In the way of laughter with freedom!
So that 'our soul' might one day
'Dance' as those trees of beauty!
Matching winds of true worth, with a
Transparent colourful butterfly!

130
Tall Tree in the Sky

Tallest tree touching the sky!
Extends towards much
Knowledge within dark or white
Clouds that roll by...

Each giving a 'picture' of changing
Moments that might 'ease'
Our difficulties of yesterday!

New rains might 'replenish' Mother
Earth – feeding your roots and ours.

Allowing the soul of our tree to
Grow more plentiful towards
Painted sky...
Just like you!
Then hidden answers might become visible?

To our deepest questions of why?

***

Helga influence (Victorian)

131
Shadows of the Past

Let darker shadows of the past blow away…

Imagine that rainy day where
Dark clouds have now been taken
Over by the sun!

Its own heart radiates 'love' that
Burns sentiments within your heart
'You' start to discover the real you!

Needing so much to shine through…

So clean those misty windows of
Your mind, for then the
World can appear good and kind.

Allowing new shadows to reflect
With 'sun ray' giving hope for
Yourself and to those 'fallen
Shadows' of others!

132
If Crying Comes Easy

If 'crying tears' comes easy, allow
Them to 'flow' freely, when you
Are alone!

As some of 'us' were brought up to
Hide emotion… for it makes 'us'
Appear weak, far from strong!

For you know when your heart
Needs to speak!
Allowing your inner soul to
Grow! To bloom!

Other people might not 'see' your
Coloured petals, as their eyes
Always seem so very far away…

So never fear, as your own
Tears are your tears…?

Then becoming shed for a reason!

That comes 'free' to show that
'You' hold compassion and shall
Always treat life with good care!

***

Helga influence (Victorian)

11th July 1994 – Local park
Inspired to write

133
Two Roses

Just as 'two roses' might not 'appear' the same?
So 'two lovers' might not be either!
For one might stay ever sweet and innocent…?
Whilst those petals of another, might
Keep blowing away… away – searching
For another?
Leaving only broken dreams.

But as life moves on…
'One' must make way for 'new
Music' from another flower to
'Mingle' a while!

Then a 'new stronger bud' of 'true worth'
Might become full of true
Intention? That holds only 'love'
And sincerity.

More likely to grow with root colouring
Only with truth and kindness!

**

Helga Influence – Victorian

134
Horoscope

Is the horoscope fortune telling?
Only you can find an answer to that!
For some days you might feel
Under the weather and need
A little sunshine under your hat!
For comforting words might tell
You to buy something new
To stop you feeling blue!
Then guilt set inside your
Heart makes you accept this
Is not 'the just' thing to do!

For we would 'all' soon run out
Of money if we went for the easy way out!
So the next best thing to get
Troubles moving… is to clear
Your mind with a friend; and
Remember not to shout!
As nothing is gained by shouting
Unless that temper or hurt
Needs to be set free!

Then freedom will 'allow' you
To make up your own ruling stars!
Encouraging your mind to see!
No, we don't need the aid of a
Crystal ball or tea leaves in
That empty cup!

For our future is 'written' within
Those stars of the sky!
Or the yellowness of a dainty buttercup!

No, we don't need those words of
A 'fortune teller', only guidance
From minds who 'speak' with
'Wisdom and truth'
So trust in the good Lord Almighty
Then!
Added sunshine shall lighten
Up your lonely life!

Reflecting out towards you!
Is all the proof you need?

135
Dreams Can Come True

Why do dreams come into our hearts?
They turn and turn into a
Pulp that cannot become 'extracted'
Or 'used' because we feel that
Dreams are only for others?
So we tend to hold onto them;
Thus we feel a suffering with pain
We take it 'inwardly' and cannot let go…

Is it because of childhood memories?
Perhaps 'they' weren't worth much!
For isolation – lack of conversation
With cuddles, those simple things
Of life; leaving only despair and
Worthlessness that become 'apparent'
When we feel sad… then withdraw
Into ourselves – fighting hard to
'Escape' from 'hurt and anger!

So allow yourselves each day; to ask
For strength to share.
As there are many who wouldn't let us down
Or we can talk quietly with your God!
To help 'us' awaken out of our
Little world once again.

20th July 1984
Inspired to write

136
Pretty Little Butterfly

Oh! Pretty little butterfly!
You 'flutter' around my form
You take away my moments of
Sadness and 'fears' of the coming storm!
Colours of the rainbow
You 'weave' around my hair…

A need comes for me to share
Your love – then just to
Stand – sit – or stare!

Oh! The wonder of creation!
That 'shines' from your wings…
So refined as silk!
Perfection with a kindness becomes
'Displayed' within your movements of skill!
Your spirit flies so freely with
No worry or care!

Interweaving wings, blend of music!
Dancing that secret message…
That gives 'us' much hope
And a healing!

***

1900's – Edwardian

137
Four Seasons...

Why should the four seasons of life
Become so special in our hearts?

I know!
It is because 'God' created them,
'All' in equal colour and part!

Spring time brings green pastures and
New flowers for all to see...

Summer holds within; as special
Sunshine with sky as dark as the
Deep blue sea!

Autumn brings golden leaves that
Come falling towards the ground...

Then winter holds
Many snowflakes like a whitewash
To cleanse the world of
All its nasty sounds.

Let's cup these all together in our
Hands and hearts, then pray a
Little harder every day to
Let 'God' know that we are
Grateful for his marvel and array!
Let us bless that all his fine
Creation of four seasons shall stay
Continuous for the rest of our long lives through!

138
Dear Golden Sunflower

Dear golden sunflower; open your
Smiling face towards me
Open up those caring eyes… tell
Me what you see!

For I am small, so near to the ground!

But 'you' are 'able' to reach out
To touch white clouds…
You always 'appear' so proud!
Each petal reflects with treasure
As that of the sun!

So don't ever blow away…
Allow your roots to stay part of the universe!
To stay 'admired' by me –
And everyone!

***

North American link

139
Pearl of our Soul

Some of our days… we can feel
Free and so fine!
All the world appears as an
Oyster – its pearl is forever thine!

But 'clouded vision' still 'holds' onto
Troubles of the world!
As 'they' go drifting by…

Then our heart becomes heavy!
And 'we' wonder why?

Then the pearl of our soul
Fights towards the surface…
Once again!
Shining forth – a sunbeam!
Letting 'us' know that lessons
Have become mastered.

Allowing stronger truths to remain?

***

Thailand link

140
Go Up Beyond Those Hills

Do not allow your world to stand
Still! For you can walk up, beyond
Those hills; then to look down
To see the world, as it really is?

You will notice colour vibrancy!
At an even distance… all those
People shall 'appear' as those 'ants'
Working together…

Then 'a clearer picture' shall become
That more pleasing!
For within God's quietness, the
Sun shall 'glisten' that much brighter!

Open bird wings – shall seem to 'enfold'
You, – taking you away from that loneliness.
Tops of trees shall appear softer;
Yet still strong! – for you to rest
Your weary mind, until the time is
Right for you to walk up that
Ladder of life!

But first we must kindle our
Earthly troubles with tribulations!
As 'our heart' shall have become
'Rested'! Including our own future
Thoughts to have become 'more' abundant
More loving!

141
Life Seems Such a Struggle

Life seems such a struggle if
Matters are not going right for you.

For 'you' tend to feel so alone
'You' think no one cares as you do!
Small burdens turn into a nightmare!
Your pathway never seems to clear…

Those darkened clouds appear
Forever above your head, making
'You' want to shed a tear!

Then a small bird might 'fly'
Across your path… that chirps
To let 'you know of a love'
That he openly sends
Then collects fallen crusts
From the ground… to feed to
His little friend!

His fluttering feathers give such delight!
Your worries 'needing' answers, seem
To come right!

Glistening leaves appear to shine!
Inspiring 'you' to sit quietly with prayer!

Then at last you realise you
Didn't need to suffer alone, as
'Spirit and bird kind' were always there!

142
Spiritual Truth

Shall:
Spiritual truth' become 'imminent' within
Your daily intentions?
Be it, if you're working, or it's
With children wanting to play…

For giving 'truths' from your heart
Is 'one' of the best gifts of all!

As happiness received back to 'you' –
Shall hold! – much 'laughter' with proof…
It shouldn't matter how small?

143
Burning Candle

Each flame that kindles brightly!
Is but a thought flowing…
And lovingly reaching to those
Higher depths of emotion!
Oh! How my own earthly mind
Needs to reach to higher vibrations
As that burning candle; raging
With many colours; red, blue and green!

As the golden aura sends out 'golden
Arrows' towards my own heart!
Sometimes my own flame 'needs' to
Reach out to that certain
Love of human kind…

To 'kindle' together, then to touch
'Vibrations' of the Earth!
Then our fingertips shall 'pulsate' as one!
To breathe, to flow… as the candle
Burning brightly… but lovingly!

Not as flames fighting against
The wind, but for our hearts
To entwine… with 'harmonious'
Echoes of angels, for 'truth' shall
Have become ours! Our souls
Free as those birds in flight!
Spreading candlelight, towards this world afar!

144
Sweet Roses

Just as roses resemble sweet wine
So your love held for me, gives
Out radiant sweetness…

Just as a bird sings harmoniously
In secret song!
So a never-ending rainbow shall
'Bare' your kindness, along my Earthly pathway!

Just as a 'humble bee' takes 'nectar
Love' within a flower!
So you shall ever grow with
'Abundance' that bears only
Fruits of joy!

***

Victorian link – gentleman in spirit to a love!

145
Tears/Pearls...

Of you who shed a tear of sorrow!
May you 'share' a smile for gain!
May, many 'pearls' of wisdom
Show 'fortitude'
Towards your spiritual reign.

***

One week before my breast operation and near my birthday

146
I'm Your Guardian Angel

You need to go to work on a foggy night
As you have more 'responsibility'
Now I've gone from you...
My heart likes to sing within evensong
When darker shadows pass your way...
Thy humble tree 'spreads' his branches
Into opening wings to 'protect'
You from elements of danger or harm.
Footsteps you hear, are but 'mine'
Alone; letting you know that I am ever here...
For I'm your guardian angel – I'm
Here to clear your path...
So rushing of golden leaves
Shall be but 'my wings' protecting
You – until I hear 'your key'
Opening your door!
I leave 'you' a kiss as 'you'
Shut the door behind you
For 'you' now feel safer with
Your children at home!
Wrapping and curling their toes
In a pleasurable way, as
Crackling of red, golden embers
Spark! That gold then blue; is but
'Spirit' letting you and your
Children know that many loved ones are
Very near, saying 'hello'! And as embers
Turn to ash, we 'all' say goodnight
God bless, may your dreams stay happy
And ever beautiful!

147
Let Your Crying Stop Tomorrow

Allow crying to stop tomorrow
Allow the sun to shine! Instead of
Looking for rain!
Allow 'yourself' to 'dream' along
With those clouds…
Helping you to smile as a child
Once again!
Allow your soul to stay ever
Young – so sunnier days can
Change into 'a playtime' – including
'Colour' from hearts' content!

So that 'the tapestry of your life'
Can become 'cherished' – then
'Woven' with 'the love' that 'spirit'
Freely sends!

148
Peace of Mind

Peace of mind, I now draw
Towards myself – with the tranquillity of it all!
Softness of sea breeze – matches 'ebb
Of tide' – that keeps its distance…
Not! Getting my feet wet?
Seagulls are hovering over the
High seas; trying to catch 'fish'
That are bobbing their heads
Up and down – glimpsing the show of sky!

Fine salt air mixes with finer, more
Delicate aromas around me.
I intake the smell of seaweed;
It seems to 'throw' me back for a while!
At last! I sense a break in
Everyday action of a busy life that
Becomes noisy, over indulged with
Petrol fumes!

Inspiration I now hold onto, like
A magnet; with an honest
Belief that 'God' is more 'powerful'
At these precious times.
Bright sky becomes more profound!
The sky and sea seem to meet
Gently and quietly…

Its contour line becomes broken
When the red sunset sits on the edge
And becomes confident
Allowing 'us' to know of another new day.

The sun goes under us! So
Silently... as 'it' disappears
From view... allowing another part
Of this world to have freedom
Of seeing it too!

Dark sky and moon 'gleams' over
With colour – and gives the opportunity
For us to shut down for the day.
So that flowers with nature
Can take a short nap... as
We all must rest at some time
Until...
Morning awakes! Many birds are
Singing... giving us pleasure for
Newness within our days...
And with much humbleness – we
Say 'a big thank you'!

149
In a Moment's Notice

In a moment's notice, when the sun dies down...
Everything around 'lights up' with
An orange glow.
Then when 'tides' are calm...
Catching orange sky dances with
Black silhouettes – vibrating with
Smaller kinds of butterfly wing!
Delicate buttercup!
Enlightening our own hearts with
Magic – 'lighter' with song!
Allowing us to smile the coming night away...
Then the white rounded moon
Carries on into day... encouraging a
Sky lark to take over singing
Happy! As 'we' watch
Different bird kinds awaiting a
Bluer sky yet to smile! Within a
Newer days' theme...
Our thoughts are no longer way out
Dreams, it seems, when sunset shall
Meet a new sunrise glow; sharing
Its own patterned golden silhouette
With white cloud blessings!

150
Golden Moon

Golden moon, you extend so high!
And appear so cold!
'Your halo' touching our shadow that
Is 'grey' and feeling old?

When 'moon' has fallen under 'that
Line' of the land and sea...
We can again 'hide' in darkness away from reality!

For deep set within our heart, we
Need to become anew! And
'Pleasing' to sight!

So we ask: golden moon, when
Your night awakes again – 'protect'
Our 'solemn shadow' under the
Wing of your light!
Then upon those hills and
Plains together... we shall
'Dance' again! Like you...
With matching stars twinkling bright!
Then our image shall not 'appear'
Grey or old any more.
For your own reflection shall 'relax'
Upon the shore!

Our soul shall have the need to follow...
For drifting moonlight shall 'ease' our
Minds clear!
Inspiring 'us' to touch coming light
With a new day.
Shedding our 'olden' shadows away...

151
Quietness

Wonderful quietness, you blend
Into our soul!

Tears return to our own eyes
Not! From feeling sad, but from
'Inspired' moments to help us
Reach our goal?

That goal that might give a picture
To where our own heart yearns to go…
The needs to love and to grow!

Taking away that heavy feeling
That's like a stone! Within
Our heart.

Made us feel 'unwanted'… Our
Identity was far from strong.

For our secret love for creation
Shall never die?

For 'spirits' are as close to us
As those birds of the sky!
Relaxing… taking shelter within
High shaded trees!

Confirming that 'courage' is forever near…
When true quietness reigns!

***

Edwardian link

179

152
Two Sides to Every Story

There are two sides to every story;
So listen with time and good care
Do not take sides even though 'you'
Know who may be right?

Just look into the heart of the
Weaker one and give a blessing
Sincere and true!
Then lend a hand to halve their
Problem, never to turn them away…

If their mind seems closed and
Wanting to go astray… 'pray'
For their soul… allowing colour
To blend with their own!
For an 'olden image' can change
Into that heavenly light!
Secretly blending in harmony with trust!

Then 'they' might have the need to
'Open' up their minds; encouraging
Olden worries… eventually to fade…
For their glimpse into their sad lives
Shall speak of something changing!

But you won't need to give your
Secret away… for you did what
Your heart chose to do!

***

Victorian link

153
I'm Sorry

My solemn heart is pounding!
As my olden thoughts are drowning!
With 'remembrance' of missing you!

I know now I didn't deserve the
'Love' you gave; for I never
'Knew' what true love was?
But I do now, as 'my soul' makes
Its way to the peacemaker, within heaven!

When I am 'accepted' within their spiritual light!
I shall shower their 'gold' upon you!

So your saddened heart may
Become filled with new joy!

Goodbye sweetest love, maybe
One day we shall meet again!

Your heart shall know it is 'me' upon
The Earth plain again, for 'my
Spirit' shall be close by your favourite tree…
Near to the old wooden gate
Where we had our first date!

When we once 'printed' you and
Me forever; that we shall
Always love and adore!

***

Husband in spirit to his wife upon the earth

154
Laughing Children

There should always be a place in 'this
World' for laughing children
Allowing innocent eyes to 'speak' with
Warmness from their hearts!

Hearts that need to stay young
Forever free!

That's if 'worldly matters' do not
'Pierce' their own reasons for
Staying loving and whole!
For it's 'us', the older ones
Who always think 'we' know it
All! Sometimes didn't defend
Them when 'they' become frightened
Or 'appeared' small!

Santa Claus or a teddy bear might
Be all that was 'allowed'
To bring 'comfort' if that 'helping
Hand' was never there to wipe
Their shedding tears…
As putting money in their hand
Instead of 'security' can only
Bring in that emptiness!
Leaving 'them' with sorrow!
Like someone saying 'goodbye'
Without reason as to where or why?

Having to grow up faster within
Their time! For 'they' must
Remain quiet! If mummy or daddy are shouting or…

For all 'they' can do is look in; from
The outside... suppressing what
'They' really feel within...
Then accept blame upon their
Young shoulders; as 'they' strive
Towards the big world alone!

If only 'children' could be regarded
As friends and not just
As a piece of property?

For it's only through dreaming that
Helps pulls then away from harsh reality!
Even though laughing dirty faces
Might belong to the child next door!

But 'deep' within their little minds
They know 'a time' shall become
Theirs – when their own offspring
Shall stay 'free' as that child should be?
To mix with all class and creed
Echoing – happiness with laughter!
Giving opportunity... to fill every
Corner of the world!

155
Ray of Sunshine

I ask for a ray of sunshine to
'Blend' within your heart!
To give 'you' strength when
You are weak… then for
'Colour' to play a part?

Sincerity with hope – I ask for you;
For all the kindness you have shown
And may 'your spirit' become
Rewarded with healing – love – and light!

Caressing those angels of heaven!

***

Victorian link

156
How Tall Are My Trees

Become as tall as the trees, and
As green as those valleys!
Take in the air to breathe
That touches the skyline of blue!

Look at the sun so bright! So tender
Spiritual awakening is forever
With us, and 'God' is forever giving
Us all 'His' splendour!

He holds us upright to the
Heavens above, and we are
Always to be His children!

Protection all around… holding
Warmth and compassion!

So when 'you' ask how tall are
My trees, how green are my valleys?

Walk towards God… then you
Shall know.

And may your pathway become
A wider road;
Forever holding its peace!

***

Gwen, a Welsh inspiration

157
I'm Free in The Sky

I'm high up in the sky!
I don't know why?
I can 'see' white daisies flying!
With a beautiful honey bee; with golden wings!
Enjoy a song with a blue bird balancing
Upon a washing line
For now my heart is set free!
Free of all pain!
Free of all sorrow – it's like there
Are no tomorrows...
Just 'my spirit' acting young again!
No more stuck in that bed, with
'Confused matter' falling into my head,
No more bricks falling on to
The ceiling – no black dots dancing in my eyes.
I'm just 'singing' with those blue birds
Oh! It's lovely, just looking down
On all my lovely friends!
Especially my sweet daughter
I'm so happy to be free!
Free to wander, to 'dance' down
Memory lane... dancing with a
Handsome man wearing a grey suit with
A small carnation! Oh, to be young
Again! No more pain.
Just wonderful golden rain!

***

Passed to spirit, 19th August 2005

I was talking and listening to a lady in the next bed. She was very ill, and obviously passing to spirit – I hope I helped her go in peace.

She passed the next morning.

158
New Found Angels

Bless the new found angels; herald
The new born king!
Rejoice 'hallelujah' open up to sing!
Stretch out your loving arms
To 'welcome' and adorn!

Notice extra love 'held' within
A star! Within night sky!
Giving 'peace' to God's children...
Encouraging souls to smile
Through... touching the coming morn!

159
Beauty of the World

Our free will becomes left to 'mingle'
With the coloured spectrum of the
Universe, as our own hand can
Become that paintbrush!
For our own thoughts can start
To stay part of those vibrations
That help make this world go round…?

For what becomes left at the end
Of a perfect day, rests upon mankind…

To what He has given back in
The way of appreciation, of how
'One' now sees beauty of those
Forgotten leaves!

Then to hold more 'compassion'
Towards the morrows, and its
Future to be!

***

Strong poet influence at Epping Forest

160
Ominous Cloud Passing

As an ominous cloud is passing – colour
Blue 'peeps' in with a confidential smile
Pushing the impending storm further away…
Allowing a lullaby to take ease within our day!
Vibrating, pulsating picturesque
Beats… instead of beating grey rain,
With a venomous storm!
Taking over sunken earth; where
Deep puddles meet – clinging onto life,
Amongst sodden roots or seeds…
Not worrying or scurrying –
Until night beckons different clouds;
Encouraging luscious green
Luminous fruits; once tomorrow's
Sunshine welcomes that hello!
Echoing with its glory!
Elevating 'discouragement' with pain
That might have been?
If a tormented 'grey cry' had taken hold!
Taking away our freedom, our choice!

***

Poet of high esteem (New inspirer)

161
The Butterfly (Blue)

Long lost love, came dancing back to
Me, when sensitive blue butterfly wing
Helped take away life's sting, as well
As the heartache it brings…

Allowing sullen hearts to 'mingle'
With a spectrum of mandarin or
Spangled gold opaque wings!

Skimming a delicate daisy or buttercup
With a slight kiss upon our cheek!
Allowing us to know that 'nature'
Ever 'grows' with us in mind;
Staying ever part of universal creativity!

***

A blue butterfly kept coming to me within my mind's eye or a
dream.
Could be the spirit of my brother Eric?

162
Melody of Sweetness

A melody of sweetness shall come to
You in the way of those fallen golden leaves!
Then you can pick them up, to
Form a pretty picture just for you!

As each 'resonating colour' shall
'Dance' and fuse together…
Your own heart can then start
To sing with a joy, with extra happiness
That shall be 'peeping' just around the corner!

Until 'new coming winds' shall blow away
Comforting leaves of playtime!
Encircling your lonely form;
Symbolising new growth yet to come!

Magical music similar to that
Of a merry-go-round, shall take
You by storm!
Then 'calming tenderness' shall
'Embrace' your mind, away from
Confusion – as 'sunshine' shall
Break through those 'discerning
Clouds', bathing 'you' with orange
Light; laced with gold!

Then a purple daisy swing shall be
There, to take 'your spirit' towards
Those 'higher heights' of heaven!

Taking you back to being a
Small child, running up towards
Those sweeping valleys, those comforting
Green hills…

A sense of belonging, shall become
Yours whenever golden leaves
Start twirling with song!
And shall become 'your secret'
For evermore, amongst a melody of sweetness!

***

I used to go on a swing at Highbury Fields.

163
Pearl of Wisdom

What day do we 'remember' the most?
Is it when we are growing up
Into an adult; or when we have that first child?
Their little hand reaches out, encouraging 'us' to smile!
Worth much more than our pure gold
Or do we link to the day; when we
Have 'settled' very quietly; started to
'Look' within ourselves, for the very first time?
Discovered 'that godliness' – we didn't know existed!
Encouraging 'our spirit' to ever reach
Out towards 'that love' with a certain
Lesson, that had become 'apparent' within
A time of sadness or insecurity!

Then a need to give out 'prayer'
For 'our blessings' to stay with 'us'
For the rest of our lives.

As knowledge came within 'one pearl'
Placed within that big vast ocean!
"For 'one' to discover! It had become
'Placed' and waiting there;
Just for you!"

***

Thailand link

164
There Is...

There is no 'harmony' as true love and peace!
There is no 'sweetness' as the 'perfume' of a rose!
There is no 'beauty' as those blues of the sky!
There is no 'happiness' as 'the joy' within children's eyes
When we 'see' the future before us;
Lighting up our faith!

165
Needing a Family

Who will be my 'guiding star' today?
You might 'appear' as that star,
So filled with light!
Burning bright!
Or 'hidden' behind darkened shadow?

Shall 'you' pass silently… within
That cold breeze?

For my empty hand shall need to stretch out!
Similar to a bird migrating to
Distant lands – to find clearer
Waters to sustain 'oneself'.
To glimpse paradise; with a caring
Family… to eventually call
My own!

***

Arab link
(Feeling very unhappy with life, with a family which
I never felt part of as a child).

1 6 6
We Are – We Can

We are those setting suns…
We are those stars of the sky!
Our souls can become 'free'
As many birds of colour with song!
We can hold strength and courage
From the magic of that tree!
Our thoughts can spare moments
To 'link' with passing clouds…
Then with brightness and humility
We can 'portray' towards others,
Depending on what person
We have now become?

***

Philosophy

167
May Peace Reign

May peace reign forever within your heart!
May love 'conquer' all hidden pain!
May 'the love of God' forever be with you...
Might all our living hours
Become 'blessed' with 'thy holy spirit'.

For we all 'need' to be of
Service to all mankind!

168
Awakening Heart

Pink carnations
Sleeping under 'yellow moon', until
Dawn paints…
An orange sky!
Then 'awakening heart' is reminded
That flowers of great magnitude
Become reborn!

Vibrating 'compassion with love'
When it is missing; within a
Lonesome soul!

***

Helga influence

169
Prayer of Faith

Within our worst moments of a quiet hour!
We feel so alone, so empty!
"And wonder: why were cuddles or
Communication 'left out' of our lives?"

For with negative shadows we can
Only 'wait' for the 'morning sun' to kiss us!

So that we might start to feel
'Whole' with 'independence' again!
Then our hands shall automatically
Fold into prayer!
Confirming
That our faith
Shall never ever leave us!

***

I have always held faith, to keep me 'going'.

170
Blessing in Disguise

Life is such a struggle when you feel so alone!
But can seem 'a blessing in disguise' when;
'New courage' becomes part of your understanding...
You shall notice nature fairies
Hiding under a bush, your favourite tree!
They hold their magic wand to
Help brighten your soul!

Then for you to wish for, that
Certain happiness – within an unexpected day!
You will 'see' a golden bridge, ready
For you to cross!

Encouraging 'you' to walk calmly
Over to its other side...

For 'that lonesome stranger' could be
Looking so patiently... waiting for
That beautiful person –
Just like you!

171
Pink Petals

Favoured heart to dream?
For when I close my eyes to
'Study' a leafy glade!
Your image still 'smiles' back to me.
Then treasured branches talk to my
Feelings; so I could take home a 'memory'
Of our sacred friendship!
That shall always stay special!

For that's when you walked upon my
Pathway when you did?
Leaving pink roses where 'your
Footprints' once stood…

A legacy of 'perfumed petals'
Whenever my own heart is
Still crying; with missing you!

***

In memory of Reg whom I knew, he always gave me a pink
rose on a tea tray. He passed to spirit in 1988.

172
Enjoy!

Enjoy the chase...
While the heart is young.
Enjoy the day – as it could pass you by?
Enjoy brighter colours to help 'hidden'
Passion, come to the fore!
Enjoy that smile – that someone special might give!
Enjoy sacred warmth that comes within hands touching!
Enjoy pleasant laughter together!

For just as music with nature
Encourages, your own heart to sing!
You can enjoy... tenderness
That becomes spoken – when two hearts
Start to beat as one!

173
Trying to Write

When all there is, is loud music in the
Making; surely it has its own place!

For when poets or writers need 'certain
Vibrations' to write 'romance' or of
'Nature kind', one has to come away
With your head feeling like wood,
Feeling in a spin!

Instead of endearment with happiness!

Then 'reminders' with the horrible odour
Of twirling grey smoke surrounding
'My aura' – instead of images
Of beautiful faces of angels.

Erasing 'once inspired thoughts', I
Shall just have to close my
Notebook to find 'creative energy'
Within another day!

For a 'ray of light' shining through the
Open door, encourages me to
Break free…

From this 'closed coffin' I feel
I am now in?

***

I used to go for lunch and take some writing with me.

174
Happiness, Never Thought Possible

Life seems such a struggle, when
Loneliness takes hold of you
But can show as a blessing
In disguise, when you allow
'Courage' to become part of your
New understanding?

For you shall notice light reflecting
Within that darkest corner!

Then spirit will 'wave' their magic
Wand – to brighten and heal your day!

For 'their silver dust' is now
Falling… allowing new love to
Blossom within.

Then 'new found reason' gave
'New aspired thoughts' touching
That 'spangled sky' within a moment's dream!

Towards happiness, you never
Thought possible

***

Philosophy

175
Pretentiousness Can Ride Away

Our soul rests within a summer's day!
Many things that seem 'pretentious'
Can ride away… with the day's cloud.

Maybe our aching heart can become renewed
For tomorrow, kindness might be
Waiting with extra happiness!

And whatever 'new fate' has to offer?

For then we might be 'able' to give
That extra smile! Then wait a while
To 'confirm' with 'God' for 'His'
Praise and understanding!

For with extra patience, loneliness
Might be at its end!

So we might start to rest our
Mind, with the 'new coming season'…

Accompanied with birds' wing!
And bonny butterfly!

176
Wake From Night's Dream

We so need moving clouds to caress us,
So we might wake from night's dream!
Feeling warmth of passion, warming kisses;
Our own emotions dancing with their
Touch! Sweeping like velvet.

For just as a rose needs to become
Reminded; that its perfume shall
Ever stay beautiful!
So our own heart can hear 'those
Sacred words'!
Sacred moments!

So that we might sleep awhile!
Then before we wake?
The colourful morning shall remind us that
Another dawn has passed!

And that our loyal pretty birds
Are in song!

***

Edwardian link

177
You Are

You are my pebble within life's ocean…
You are my sand beneath my feet.
You are that breeze that whispers many thoughtful words!

You have become my true love, as
Never before experienced…?
You held my hand when comfort
Was needed – as before I used to
Be so alone!
Life as it should have been seemed
To be pulling away from me.
'Your spiritual face' helped make
My sun that brighter!
I'm no longer afraid; when it's
Thunderstorm or rain! For
You are that coloured leaf, that
Was needed to 'nurture' my earthly tree?
Helping to find that 'one piece'
Of jigsaw missing… that only left me
With that 'gnawing' within my heart!
At last an end of visualising
'Prince Charming' maybe on that white horse!
For 'reality' came when 'God' left
Me with a legacy – a promise!
That 'all' shall become well
When 'another soul' shall soon
See 'my hidden light'!
Eventually entwining two lost souls!

True story!

178
Different Pathway

Many have experienced
Broken hearts!
Broken dreams!
It seems!
For 'plans' we held for yesterday
Could not come to fruition.

For some days our partner lets us
Down in so many ways.
Or has other plans, to do extra time
At work, holding more responsibility
With different tasks!
As we can walk upon different
Pathways – different levels at
Different times.

So our own days can become more
Pleasing to do something for ourselves
Sharing with nature, the
Trees; with many leaves that fall!

My own day became 'spent' when
An uplift came unexpectedly;
Sitting by river echoes…
Helping my pen to 'flow' much more
Freely – with 'new inspirational' moments
Scribing into my pages!
Pushing tearful times aside!

***

Someone let me down.

179
Battling Alone

Looking out of a pub window, sitting on my own;
Drinking coffee – just had lunch
Brightens me up, lifts my spirit!

'Sun ray' shining through the glass
Reminding us that we are never
Really alone, although many tears
Well up within our throat – our heart's centre!

So it seems today is another dark
Day – tomorrow might become brighter!

For if we hold strong faith – we
Might write or paint.
So we shouldn't appear too ungrateful
For creative blessings we have!

As spiritual benefits can become more
'Apparent' through darkness within a
Moment's misery?

But birds with butterflies dancing!
With healing green, magical stem
Or tree... can give to you
That song within!
Giving courage with more belief
Within yourself!

180
Fairy and Gnomes

As we dance and frolic amongst
Daisies and green fields, we lift
Our hearts high up to those
White clouds!

We seem to drift on air… as
'Our souls' are taken towards heaven!
We touch colours of those higher
Vibrations and much warmth is
Flowing – so freely…

Small buds are 'opening' their centres
To become as a playground…
Fairy and gnome-like creatures
Act out their fantasies…for
Their perfection, for simplicity
Is so much to be desired!

Everything around us becomes so
'Light and so true' with 'radiance
Of smiles' everywhere!
No worries or perplexities
Just laughter!

As we 'catch' beams of sunshine
That 'draw' from their faces!
'They' hold out their hands
To greet us; and 'we' all
Become as children…
Sense of time is not with us;
Only a joy!

For Earth life 'awakens' us again
For 'reality' plays an important
Part for 'we' are surely
'Strengthened' from this
Turning of event; as it
Can become used in
Helping others!

***

My friend Gwen's influence within a dream.

1 8 1
Compassion for Life!

I always hold a 'romantic heart…'
But 'sullen grey' kept haunting me;
Through lack of emotional love!
'Despair and hopelessness, until
'Mirrored reflection' – became entwined
With forests, birds or flowers!
Where 'my soul' needed to reach
Outwards… to become a part?
For only then did I feel safe!

For 'God' spoke freely within 'spectrum
Shade…', colour green gave me courage
Held me strong! Within my disability?

'Inner faith' always followed me…
Encouraging 'me' to speak with compassion!
Even though I often felt so alone!

But since I met you, Alan my life became
That much sweeter; as I could sense
'You' came with humbleness.
Holding hands was not just a wish
Coming true… but became a reality!
My own hopes and desires able to
Grow that much stronger!
Making our tree of life! Root! With
A togetherness!

***

Met 'Alan' at a singles' club, 11th June 2006

182
Sad Memory

Pictures of candles painted upon a card;
Red poppies dancing within a yellow
Field! Resembles
Happiness maybe?
But beautiful images; only gave me pain!
Symbolising red rain…!
Beating within my heart!

Instead of warming kisses with
Smiles 'you' once had only for me!

***

Personal link: 'R'.

183
Keep Forever True!

Keep forever true and humble thou art
Accept that 'you' are 'receiving'
What 'you' are seeking?

Total freedom with peace – is
All around... for 'you' to
Take in within your soul being!

As honesty with 'self-sacrifice'
Becomes rewarding... for any
Weakened heart!

For strength with courage 'becomes'
Your master!
When that certain aim finally...
Becomes a very important part!

184
Was it So Wrong?

Was it so wrong to love you?
Was it so wrong to have needed to stay close?
For warming kisses with you 'dearest one'
Was like 'sharing' a perfume of sweet roses!

Each moment of time 'shared' seemed
To pass so quickly – became so precious!

Until those goodbyes had to become
Said as 'sacred time' passed with
Emotional tears, still keeping within!

My days; those months were very
Hard to bear! But with sunrise;
Those sunsets – helped me to keep
Smiling! Until 'our day' came closer
To sharing a momentous heart again!

***

My experience

185
Spiritual Bridge

Clasp your hands together, thank
The good Lord in prayer;
Touch! The pink glowing clouds
Around you, then visualise your
Own temple there!

Know that 'it' will await you when
Your journey is to come; to take
A step into the other world, that
You can call home.

And may your own 'spiritual bridge'
Be as strong as you have built it!

***

I saw mentally a pink bridge within a dream.

186
Poppy of Beauty, Not War!

As I sit with a lonely poppy 'rooted'
To a border's edge;
I gather in a store of beauty as
A robin flies to a nearby hedge.
His little eyes rest very still…
As if to wonder!
Should I trust?
Or do I scamper? To the safety of a tree?

Just then! the poppy so radiant;
So proud!
Seemed to speak out loud
"Take time to look within my
Tissue like petals as I am
A red poppy made with 'creator's'
Hands for all to see!"

Not just to recall sad times
Of 'Remembrance Day' when I
Am used as a symbol
To commemorate the pains of war!

What suffering 'the end product'
Entails when it has to be
'Equalled' out! To bear and to share!

Mothers, wives and children are
Left to ponder! Cry or stare!
We might ask why!

Why do we need to let hate with
Strong anger take over?
To watch planes 'dog fight' in the sky?

Can all be forgotten?
When medals or an epitaph is
Written with courageous words;
As courage I feel, should
Come from a kind heart
Talking peace with love – not!
From the bitterness of tongues;
Fighting! Like two swords.

Then the colour of the poppy
Would not be 'painted' with
Blood and terror!
And the trusting eyes of
That little robin would
Stay, forever!

So let us strive on, for something
Sweet and new!
As the creator would wish that too!

Then the seeds of the poppy could
Fly free! To dance in the
Country with 'abundance' of joy!
Could 'become sown' to finally
Get us through!

Then the heartbeat of the
Robin would be felt on the
Palm of our hand...

So we can all laugh and venture together!
To marvel at God's skill
Set on his 'arable lands...'

***

Inspired to write, at Hopton-on-Sea, Sussex.

187
Star Adorning

Don't hide behind that shadow;
Come out and 'catch' the light!
Like a star adorning above you;
Your own beauty shining so bright!
It might seem far, far away…
But the 'star' needs to become
'Recaptured' and 'adored'.
Just as 'the universe' likes to
Become explored – for evermore!

***

188
Hidden Love

Allow me to 'discover' the warmth of your love!
Before 'you' fall away from me?
Allow your own 'heartbeat' to 'beat' with my own!
Allowing 'my soul' to 'touch'
Your tenderness… that colours
So secretly from you!
As
The glow within your eyes, shine
As 'magic' releasing from
Your inner soul!

Such 'being' needing to 'express'
To nurture!
So much emotion, hidden within
Depths… that go very deep!

My own experience.

189
Star of Light with Hope?

Star of light!
Star of hope!
Do not abandon us when in dire need.
Spread your light to touch 'our'
Hidden facets, that long
To reach towards a happiness –
Towards a love!

In return we shall one day 'express'
Our ardour for you;
When our own points of the star
Shall 'touch' your very own;
Then we can help brighten
And lighten all those corners
Of the world together!

***

190
Why Do We?

Why do our feet feel sore from
Treading this pathway of ours?
Why can't we 'tread' those grapes
Of sweetness – for our minds to
Become clearer as those healing
Waters of the ocean? To experience
Happiness of that swaying tree.
To hold 'new expectations' with the
Blueness of blue sky!
Colouring 'us' with confidence as
That of the sun!
Spreading its own beauty of
Light! Performing miracles of
Discovery!

Why can't we discover who 'we' are?
Why do we have to learn those
True colours of our being –
Through tolerance
Pain and
Injustice!

191
Freedom of Heart

Freedom of heart, where are you?

No light within our eyes! Why do you not shine?

Colour of our lips – why do you not blossom red?
Conveying happy words to say?

Why do we have to experience
Untouched love. No hand
To touch our own within life's crisis?

What cross to bear?
What suffering do we need to
Go through to prove we can
Survive those rough waters…?

Before sunrise becomes due to
Uplift our hearts,
Allowing its warmness to
Colour our lips!

Encouraging 'new opened eyes' to
'See' written words, 'skimming'
The sky! So high! That says…

All will be well!
That peace with a love, shall 'shower'
Upon you all!

***

Chinese link

192
Have You?

Have you ever sat under the
Beauty of a weeping willow tree?
Have you ever sat upon green
Grass; allowed 'it to dance...
Between your free toes?
Have you ever 'discovered' emotion
That's portrayed within a yellow rose?
Have you ever become 'healed'
By the pool of healing waters?
Or become guided by those
Stars of a night sky?
Then listened and spoke with
Nature – the way that animals do?
For 'they' know that 'creativity'
Shall always 'grow' with the kindness of man!
Portraying, sharing towards me –
Towards you
Helping to make this world a far better place?
Encouraging your empty dreams
To become 'filled with the
Wonder of an 'arched rainbow theme'!

193
So Much Beauty

The sun…
The moon…
Those stars…

So much beauty to behold!
So much splendour within
Those living grasses!

'Mystical shadows' within all
Rivers… echoing much colour…
Enriching our blood; to help
Maintain
True self-worth!

For we are but living seeds
Still… yet to grow!
Into magnificent beautiful trees!

***

Chinese link

194
Music and Beauty!

Those stars 'shine' ever so brightly!
When we link with music.
Flowers of our garden speak more
Radiantly, when our heart beats
With their own…

God's trees appear taller, touching the sky!
Taking away 'our greyest moments'
To link with an 'inspiration theme'.

Aspiring us to reach out towards
'Inspirational love' that we know
Is there!

For the echo of God's sun, helps us to
Stay free of physical or mental pain
So we may dance with the sweet butterfly!

Sharing outspan wings with secrets…
'Hiding' within earthly mists!

Awakening our own minds, to all
Known living beauty within this:
Thy beloved universe!

195
Mum!

Thinking of pink shadow within your sky!
Gave me a memory of you;
Painted blue, reminded me of
Tears that you 'once' shed!
Not wanting to let go!

But God had other plans
'You' are now comforted
Under his golden wing!
Took away your inner pain!

Only your sweet smile with
Caring vibration remained!
Still colouring every person
With your humbleness so true!

For your spirit Mum!
Shall always be around;
Towards 'those' who cared.

For we 'all' shall never, ever
Forget you!

***

My mum, Margaret (Maggie)

1 9 6
Xmas Shared

Xmas!

Just around the corner…
Lots of gifts to wrap!

Chocolates with mince pies, helps
To make 'one' smile!

Aroma of turkey, potatoes, red
Jelly – different wines, inviting!

But do not ever allow ourselves
To forget the lonely, the
Forgotten, the hungry!
The poor of this world!

Allow us all to 'share' to 'care'
With free tokens of thought with love!
For us to stay ever thankful
For what 'we' have!

Then with 'free will' on our side
We can display 'healing' from
Warming hearts…

Uniting together, forever!
With 'charity' and prayer!

197
Reminiscing with an Old Man

Sitting alone in my old rocking chair;
I ponder with the past…
With happiness as well as those tears!

I become 'reminded' of many children
I've known through those years.
As I look and stare at the old
Flamed fire, burning in the grate…

I give prayer with thanksgiving, amongst
Loyalty and hate?

But at the end of the day, I know
I have been 'protected' with
The love I now recall!

For to have faith in Mother Earth;
Those beautiful stars!

Is the most wondrous gift of all!

***

Old man speaking of his life

25th December 1982 – Christmas Day – woke up to a symbol of a
snowflake upon my curtain
Inspired to write

198

Snowman

(From an old playmate)

Come winter time, I shall be in the snow;
Make me into your snow friend
And I shall be with you wherever you go!

Give me pebble eyes that I may see!
You can talk with me of olden dreams…
Build me up, build me high!
So you can climb on me to touch the sky!

Put a scarf around to keep me warm.
Place me under a tree, to give me
Comfort from the storm…
My 'footprints' shall be shown
Deep in the ground!
Please put your footprints in
'Mine', you shall feel me safe
And sound.

Blue sky shall be happy times, we
Shall dance in the yellow sun,
And our footprints shall melt into rain!
But you shall 'see' my reflection
In a puddle once again.

Please do not ever think of me
As gone! For I shall show in
The colour of the rainbow…

Then flowers will come through
The hard earth, you will
'Hear' my sweet hello!

I shall look at you through the
Blossom of the trees;
My hum or song will 'guide'
You through – when you seem
Lost... 'You' will know it is me.

God may have taken 'me' early
To heaven, but now all
My pain has blown away...

Angel friends and fairies play with
Me in rose gardens and a
'Light' is a love in all our days...

My young soul follows 'the spirit
Of life', wherever it needs to take me.
But my 'prayers' are always
Upon you friend, as with spirit
As there is no other place
I would rather be!

***

Victorian link
From a boy aged 9

199
Full Moon...

Rounded full moon...
You 'shine' your light across
Clouded dark sky!

So that we may 'glimpse' the magic
Of birds' wings, against the dancing
Of black silhouettes!

Twinkling stars, help us to smile!
Then to dream a while!

For you come to 'share' your
Security upon our pathway...

For then silver dust 'glistens'
Upon earthly ground!
Are but kisses from our
Loved ones in spirit!

Reminding us that 'they' are still
Watching over...

Especially when cold December
Winds blow up a storm!

200
Innocent Eyes with Xmas

Innocent eyes of children sparkle or
When 'they' open up glittered
Paper, coloured ribbons
Pulling at the sellotape!

Eager to know what Father
Christmas has left them?
Their own imagination... dancing
With noisy toys, cuddle teddy
Bears; reflecting their own joy!
Their personality!
With their Christmas time!

Great happiness, parents or
Grandparents, would not
Want to miss!
Or ever to pass them by...

201
Market Day

Wavy leaves 'echo' with a magical gleam!
So we may enjoy our day!

For 'it's' market time, many stalls
Displaying trinkets, clothes of a
Warmer kind, striped scarves,
Long leggings, preparing for
Winter moments.
Blended with harsher winds
Affecting our fingers, our toes…

But white shaded sun is momentarily
Kind, hot coffee cups keeping our
Hands warm; amongst jolly music
Being played!

Clinking of a charity box…
Encouraging 'us' to stay humble!
As we link to 'others' much
Worse off than we!

Realising shared moments' pleasures,
Becoming so sacred!
As the *Big Issue* is trying to
Become sold, pie and mash shop nearby…

Waltham Abbey clock chimes! As
We pass the coloured fruit stall!

Must stop at the Victorian Tea Shop,
Old fashioned teapot with cup
And small milk jug, buttered bun to hand!

Must buy some Xmas cards, ribbons
With glittered paper!
Sharing our shivery smile as 'we'
Acknowledge amongst strangers with children!

That 'Xmas Day' is just around the corner!